COLORADO ON FOOT

COLORADO ON FOOT

by Robert L. Brown

Maps by Dolores Peterson

The CAXTON PRINTERS, Ltd.
Caldwell, Idaho
1994

First printing June, 1991
Second printing November, 1994

Brown, Robert Leaman, 1921–
Colorado on foot / by Robert L. Brown.
    p.   cm.
ISBN 0–87004–336–6 : $9.95
Hiking--Colorado--Guide-books.   2. Colorado--
Description and travel--1981--Guide-books.   I. Title.
GV199.42.C62B76   1991
917.88'0433--dc20   91-8054
                                                                        CIP

Lithographed and bound in the United States of America by
The CAXTON PRINTERS, Ltd.
Caldwell, Idaho
159658

For Jennifer Zombola,
who loves to walk, too.

CONTENTS

Acknowledgments xi

Introduction xiii

Denver and Jefferson Counties 1

    Apex and Gregory Toll Road 2
    Apex Gulch to Indian Mountain 6
    Beaver Meadows 10
    Chimney Gulch to Mount Zion 14
    Coyote, Elk and Raccoon Trails 18
    Elk, Mule Deer and Blue Grouse Trails 22
    Forgotten Valley 26
    Grass Creek and Lost Creek Trails 30
    Green Mountain and Lonesome Trails 34
    Horseshoe and Coyote Trails 38
    Maxwell Falls 42
    Mount Falcon 46
    Mule Deer and Goat Trails 50
    Roxborough State Park.......................... 54
    White Ranch 58

Boulder County 63

    Crags Boulevard 64
    Gregory Canyon and Saddle Rock 68
    Mesa Trail, South End 72
    Rainbow Lakes 76
    Switzerland Trail, Eldora Branch 80

Clear Creek and Gilpin Counties 85

    Blue Lake 86
    Butler Gulch 90

Geneva Mountain 94
Grizzly Gulch 98
Hells Hole Trail 102
Herman Gulch 106
Lincoln Mountain 110
McClellan Mountain 114
Murray Lake 118
North Empire Trail 122
Ohman Lake 126
Peak 11,704 130
Pesman Trail 134
Mount Sniktau 138
Vasquez Pass 142
Watrous Gulch 148

Rocky Mountain National Park 153

The Alberta Falls-Lake Haiyaha Circle 154
Bierstadt Lake 158
Fall River Road 162
Storm Pass 166

Colorado Springs Vicinity 169

Jones Park 170
Original Ute Pass 174
Pikes Peak 180

South Park and Vicinity 185

Alpine Tunnel 186
Ben Tyler Trail 190
Brookside Trail 194
French Pass from Breckenridge 198
French Pass from South Park 202
Hooper Trail 208
Hoosier Ridge East 212
The Iron Chest Mine Trail 216
Mount Arps 222
The Rosalie Trail 226

The Rosalie Trail from Guanella Pass 230
Rolling Creek Trail 234
Williams Pass 238

Summit County Area 243

Lily Pad Lake 244
Ptarmigan Pass 248
South Willow Creek 252
Wheeler Lakes 256

San Juan Area 261

Atlas Mine Trail 262
Clear Lake 266
Colorado Trail 270
Governor Basin 274
Kendall Mountain 278
McMillan Peak 282
Mosca Pass 286
Mount Abram 292
Silver Basin 296
Silver Lake 300

Yule Marble Quarry 305

Yule Marble Quarry Trail 306

ACKNOWLEDGMENTS

For assistance rendered during the preparation of this book, the writer wishes to acknowledge the help given by a fairly extensive number of persons, organizations, and institutions. Among the sources consulted were the Library of the State Historical Society of Colorado, the Western History Department of the Denver Public Library, and the trip records at the library of the Colorado Mountain Club.

Several books were consulted in order to cross check information about the trails. They were the following: *High Country Names* by Louisa Ward Arps and Eleanor Kingery, Sage Books, Chicago, 1972; *Guide to the Colorado Mountains* by Robert Ormes, The Colorado Mountain Club, Denver, 1979; *The Great Gates* by Marshall Sprague, Little Brown, Boston, 1964; *Colorado's Other Mountains* by Walter R. Borneman, Cordillera Press, Evergreen, 1984; and *Hiking the Highest Passes* by Bob Martin, Pruett Press, Boulder, 1984.

Once again, Freda and Francis Rizzari gave unstintingly of their time, knowledge, and skills by proofreading the completed manuscript. Their competence and many suggestions have been invaluable.

Most of the photographs used in this book were taken with a Minox EL and with a Pentax. Since the original 35mm slides were in color, copy negatives were made on Plus X film.

On February 20, 1988, Charles Smith, Senior Editor at Charles Scribner's Sons told me that "Every book is automatically out of date on the day it is published." Be that as it may. Nevertheless, last minute checks have been made concerning trail information in order to minimize errors. Inevitably, changes in trails and even in names are sometimes made by the Forest Service and others in a position to affect such alterations beyond the control of the rest of us. One example was the sudden name change in Golden Gate State Park of Blackman Meadows to Frazer Meadows. In another instance, a chapter dealing with a historic and scenic Indian trail was deleted almost at the last moment when a change in land ownership resulted in denial of further access in the foreseeable future.

Once again, as in my previous hiking book, *Uphill Both Ways*, the personal pronoun "we" appears frequently in the chapters that follow. It refers to Evelyn McCall Brown, my wife and best friend for more than four decades. She is a fine hiker and my companion on most of the outings and was responsible for many of the photographs. For many of the hikes we had as companions our good friends Berta and the late Dr. William H. Anderson. Two other close friends, Barbara and Earl Boland accompanied us on most of the walks in the lovely San Juan country and in some other localities. Others who have gone with us on one or more of the hikes include Nancy and Ed Bathke, Marian and Dick Ramsey, Nadine and Bob Muth, Elwyn and the late Louisa Ward Arps, Bob McCaig, Rev. Don Simonton, the late Rev. Eric Veal, Priscilla Hawthorne, Barbara and John Adams, Helen Kneale, Hazel Rice, Carl Blaurock, Dr. Tom Noel, and our son, Marshall Alan Brown.

To all of these lovers of Colorado's high country go our sincere gratitude for good times shared and the hope that we may enjoy future hikes in their company.

R.L.B.

AN INTRODUCTION TO
HIKING IN COLORADO

Nearly all Coloradoans share a deep affection for and an appreciation of our natural geography, in particular the vast chain of the Rocky Mountains that divides the state, east from west. Well before the beginning of serious exploration, the Continental Divide was regarded as a natural barrier. Within Colorado's boundaries there are fifty–three peaks that reach heights of more than 14,000 feet above sea level, fifty-four if you count Mount Cameron. Hundreds of others, some still unnamed, exist in the 12,000 to 13,000 foot category. There are several linear ranges in Colorado's Rockies, extending north and south, not just the single range. This condition became a source of anxiety and frustration to both official explorers as well as to those later gold rush pioneers who sought to cross the territory.

In the early years of the last century there was much curiosity about the still unnamed area that became Colorado. From the very beginning the mountains were a factor in all of the attempts to explore this land. Zebulon Pike was the first to come to what were then known as the "Mexican Mountains." The Spanish, of course, were here much earlier, but apparently they had little interest in mountaineering. Pike followed the Arkansas River toward the mountain that now bears his name. Later he entered South Park. In January the party crossed the Sangre de Cristo Range to the San Luis Valley, which was Spanish territory at that time. There they were captured and taken to Santa Fe in New Spain.

Next to come was Stephen H. Long who followed the Platte River into the territory in 1820. He mistook today's Longs Peak for Pikes Peak, using it as his beacon. Dr. Edwin James, a botanist, was the most interesting member of the expedition. James became the first American to reach the top of Pikes Peak. Major Long tried in vain to have the peak named in James' honor.

John C. Fremont crossed Colorado's mountains on each of five westward expeditions between 1842 and 1853. Almost the last to come, in 1853, was Captain John W. Gunnison, who sought a transcontinental railroad route over the Rockies. He was killed in Utah, probably by Paiute Indians, and Fremont's 1853 expedition completed the survey.

One need only to peruse Colorado's history to grasp the importance of the mountains. Today, the fascination continues unabated. This state contains some of the roughest and most scenic high country hiking to be found anywhere. More than a few of those routes followed by our earliest explorers can be hiked today and some are included in this book. Other and later trails were blazed by those who came in search of precious metals. Others built toll roads and rail lines through and over the Rockies. Some of these are fascinating trails that hikers may enjoy. Many of the other walks described within these pages were built in the present century by the U.S. Forest Service or similar agencies to enable people to reach places of scenic beauty that they might enjoy seeing.

As with any semi-strenuous activity, some common sense precautions should be observed. First, choose a pack that is comfortable, one that fits your back and shoulders. Inside it, always carry a bottle of water, light rain gear, a hat, and an extra pair of dry socks. Comfortable boots are critical. For a single day of hiking there are a number of lightweight types of footwear in the fifty dollar to one hundred dollar price range that offer both comfort and adequate support. Obviously, they should undergo break-in procedures at home, not on the trail. Be sure the boots you select are roomy enough to accommodate heavy rag socks. Be certain that they bend in the right places (where your foot bends). Many of the newer boots are lighter and easier to break in and require less upkeep. Some have uppers of Gore-Tex, which allows your feet to breathe and is also fast drying. For hikes of longer duration, heavier boots are a must. At high altitudes on steep slopes avoid the error of pushing yourself. Never compete with other hikers, only with yourself and with the peak you are climbing.

Aside from becoming lost, probably the greatest danger in high altitude hiking is an electrical storm. It has been estimated that lightning hits our earth 100 times every second. Many of these strikes occur in our high mountains where there is little protection. In Colorado most thunderstorms move from east to west and occur between noon and 2:00 P.M. If you are unable to reach your destination by noon, turn back if inclement weather threatens. Most lightning-caused deaths occur out of doors. Nearly half of all such cases happen while people are engaged in outdoor activities.

If caught in an electric storm, get off the peak, avoid high places or tall trees as lightning seeks out the highest projection. If possible, find a low area and present a low profile. Sit on your pack with only your boots in contact with the earth. If caught in an open or flat area, either squat or bend down and place your hands on your knees. Do not lie down. The idea is to present as low a profile as possible while maintaining minimal contact with the ground. As a precaution, get rid of any metal on your person or in the pack. The National Weather Service estimates that over 200 persons are killed by lightning each year. In Colorado the average has been five people annually. If possible, take cover in a grove but never by a single tree. Summer, our most desirable walking season, is lightning time. Although autumn is safer, snow squalls in August or September are no rarity in Colorado. Above all, be prepared and use common sense.

In an earlier book, *Uphill Both Ways* (Caxton, 1976), I described some of our very favorite hikes. The present volume continues, presenting other trails that we have particularly enjoyed. Evelyn McCall Brown made nearly all of these hikes with me and took many of the photographs. She appears in some of the others, including the cover picture. Without her dedication, patience, and stamina, this book would have been far more difficult.

R.L.B.

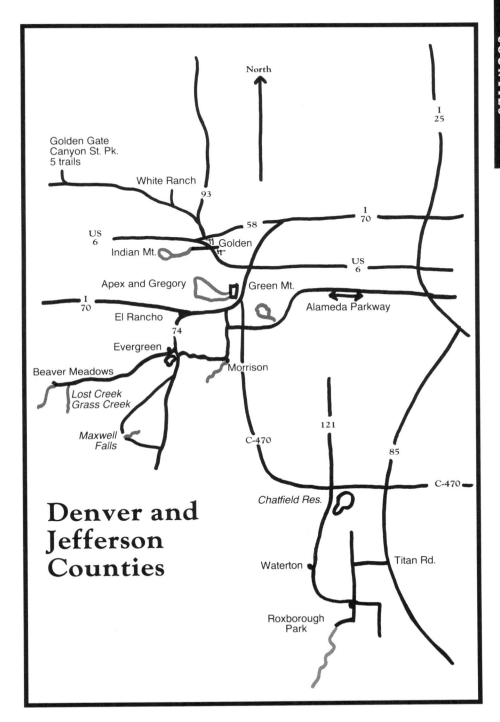

North

Golden Gate
Canyon St. Pk.
5 trails

White Ranch

93

I
25

I
70

US
6

58

Golden

Indian Mt.

US
6

Apex and Gregory

Green Mt.

I
70

Alameda Parkway

El Rancho

74

Evergreen

Morrison

Beaver Meadows

*Lost Creek
Grass Creek*

121

*Maxwell
Falls*

C-470

85

C-470

Chatfield Res.

Denver and
Jefferson
Counties

Waterton

Titan Rd.

Roxborough
Park

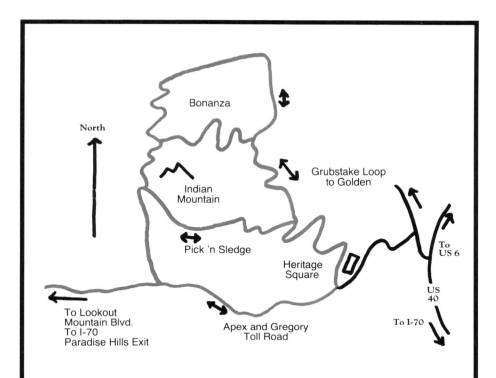

Bonanza

North

Grubstake Loop
to Golden

Indian
Mountain

Pick 'n Sledge

Heritage
Square

To Lookout
Mountain Blvd.
To I-70
Paradise Hills Exit

Apex and Gregory
Toll Road

To
US 6

US
40

To I-70

Apex and Gregory Toll Road

APEX and GREGORY TOLL ROAD

Miners who sought gold in the mountains west of Denver in 1859 are known to have hacked out at least three trails for access to the Gregory diggings near present Central City and Black Hawk. The first of these followed the spine of Mount Vernon Canyon somewhat below the present grade of Interstate 70. A second road ascended Golden Gate Canyon from the now extinct town of Golden Gate City. The third entered the mountains by way of a steep gulch between the first two trails. Called the Apex and Gregory Toll Road, it is the subject of this chapter because, unlike the other two, its wheel scars remain and it can be hiked today.

To provide for the needs of the miners, three small supply towns grew up almost in a north-south line along the eastern edge of the foothills. Golden Gate City was the most northerly of the three, located slightly north and west of contemporary Golden. It served as the most logical embarkation point for the Golden Gate Canyon Toll Road. For the nearby Mountain Vernon Toll Road, a town called Mount Vernon flourished just southwest of the point where the Morrison Hogback road passes beneath Interstate 70. Traces of the old settlement are still visible below the freeway, but much lies buried under the extensive landfill. The Mathews House and the site of Governor Robert W. Steele's cabin can still be seen.

For the Apex and Gregory road a town called Apex stood where the Heritage Square amusement park is now located. In common with its neighbor to the south, Apex likewise is buried under a huge landfill. Its emigrant trail went up the draw just west of the stable, between it and the miniature railroad. At this writing the right-of-way

3

has been acquired by the Jefferson County Open Space Program. Colored plastic strips attached to wooden posts mark it as a hiking path. From the stable, the distance up to the top is just under two and a half miles.

Along the way you will see the original rock cribbing, put in place more than a century ago to secure the road to the hillside. Since a stream traverses parts of this gully, following the easier route along the base would have been impractical. Here and there the original double-rutted scars left by iron-tired wagon wheels are visible even now.

As a hike, this one is short. Also, it is far more historic than scenic. The Apex and Gregory road was built in 1859 and was used continuously through 1865. Its abandonment was dictated by the fact that it was much steeper than its two competitors. Originally it extended up through Paradise Hills and the Mount Vernon complex before descending Big Hill into Clear Creek Canyon somewhat beyond tunnel number three. From that point it was an easy trek up Clear Creek to either Idaho Springs or to the Central City or Black Hawk areas.

Instead of taking a conventional hike, up and back on the same path, you could use two cars and hike only one way. The upper end of the trail begins at the junction of the Lookout Mountain road with Colerow Road. Leave one car at Heritage Square and the other at the Jefferson County Conference and Nature Center on Colerow Road. Walk over to the marked trailhead and start downhill.

Since this hike is a brief one, you could add to it by walking the trail in the Mathews–Winters Open Space Park. It starts at the aforementioned Mount Vernon townsite and circles the hill to the south. For any season other than winter these are short but pleasant walks that have the added virtue of being close to the metropolitan area.

The original grade of the Apex and Gregory toll road is visible from the Heritage Square trailhead when looking uphill.

A section of the old rock cribbing still supports the Apex and Gregory Grade near the railhead.

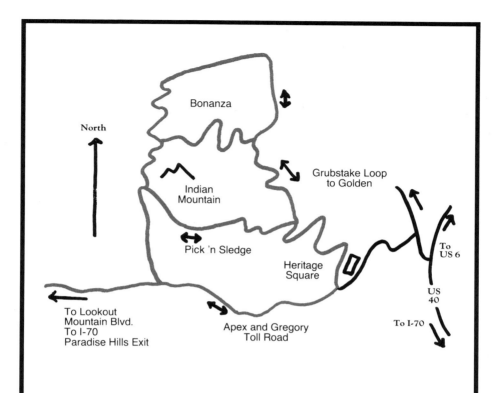

North

Bonanza

Indian
Mountain

Grubstake Loop
to Golden

Pick 'n Sledge

Heritage
Square

To
US 6

US
40

To Lookout
Mountain Blvd.
To I-70
Paradise Hills Exit

Apex and Gregory
Toll Road

To I-70

Apex Gulch to
Indian Mountain

APEX GULCH to
INDIAN MOUNTAIN

This easy climb uses the same trailhead as the Apex and Gregory Toll Road hike. Start behind the stables at Heritage Square and follow the marked Pick 'N Sledge Trail for just over a half mile. As a reminder of the days when this was an emigrant wagon road to Central City, a large sign has been placed beside the trail. Since road use was not free during Colorado's mining period, the toll fees you would have paid are posted for wagons, horses and mules, pedestrians, as well as for cattle and sheep. Although funeral processions used the road at no fee, this classification has not appeared on the sign as yet.

At the first junction take the right fork and follow Grubstake Loop for half a mile to Bonanza Trail. In late spring the flowering wild plum bushes that line this path are particularly fragrant. Quite a diverse variety of wild flowers make this a rewarding walk during the hiking season. Both deciduous and evergreen trees and an abundant growth of wild shrubbery also line this path.

When you reach Bonanza Trail, turn left or west and follow the switchbacks uphill. As you approach what is obviously the top of 7,281 foot high Indian Mountain, leave the path and bushwhack the few remaining yards to the summit. This is a heavily wooded area with plenty of shade for a picnic. Several large and halfway comfortable rocks provide places to sit while enjoying your "tea and biscuits." Because this part of the foothills tend to get little natural moisture, the vegetation and abundant pine needles are particularly prone to burning. Avoid building fires and be careful of discarded matches or cigarettes. We always pack a lunch that requires no cooking.

Below you is the town of Golden. To the east, Highway 6 leads across the low, rolling hills to Denver.

7

The winding trail on Indian Mountain is a pleasant and easy one.

Lakewood and West 6th Avenue are visible from Indian Mountain's
summit.

Now turn in the opposite direction and enjoy a nice view of the snow-capped Front Range. When you are ready to depart, return by the same route to Bonanza Trail.

To avoid repetition, go left when you reach the path and continue along down the well-worn route that traverses the west slope of Indian Mountain. Turn left at the next intersection and walk southeast down the Pick 'N Sledge Trail toward Heritage Square. When you come to Apex Trail again you will be in sight of the amusement park.

By the time you get back to your car you will have walked about four miles. The elevation gain from Heritage Square to the top of Indian Mountain is a scant 1,200 feet. Because this is a fairly low altitude hike, be noisy when the weather is warm. Snakes have been known to live in this area. Bang a walking stick on the rocks, whistle, or sing and you will probably never see a reptile.

Also due to the low altitude this trail can be hiked in all but the most inclement weather. We tend to prefer cool autumn and late spring days as the most pleasant times for an easy and pleasant stroll up Indian Mountain.

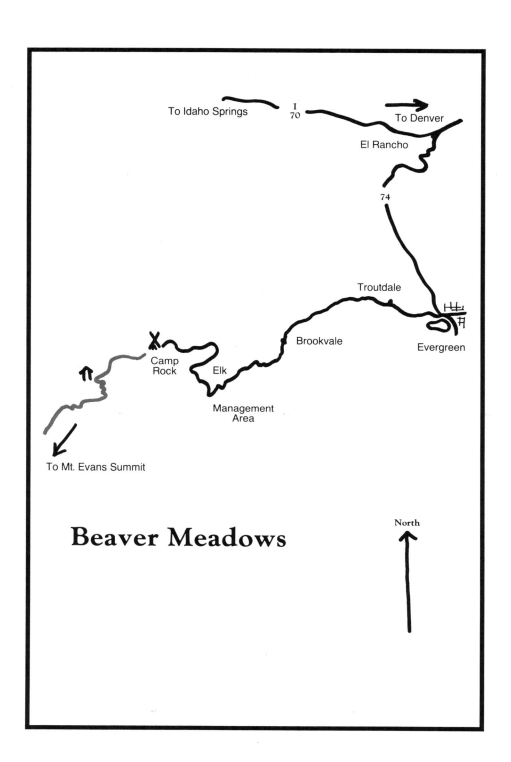

Beaver Meadows

BEAVER MEADOWS

To reach the trailhead for this hike, leave Evergreen on Colorado State Highway 74 and drive to the Upper Bear Creek Road. Continue on this road for six miles. Turn right at the junction and follow the Singing River Ranch signs for two miles to a junction. Turn left and go past the Mount Evans Elk Management building. Now the road becomes rough and a bit steep in places for the next several miles. Finally, below the road there is a marked parking area for the trail to Beaver Meadows. The trail starts from the lower end of the parking area and heads into the heavily wooded terrain of the Arapaho National Forest.

This is an easy, sheltered trail with quite modest elevation gains. It follows an attractive little creek, crosses it on a sturdy bridge, and continues up to the more open area of Beaver Meadows. Here you will find several abandoned and drained beaver lodges. The trail skirts the meadow on the right side as you enter the area. It climbs gently up to a pair of three-sided rustic shelters that have been provided for hikers.

Beyond the shelters, the path turns to the left as you near the far end of the meadow. It enters the forest once more and climbs up toward the west before turning off to the southwest. If the weather is clear you may wish to continue on this path. It leads all the way up to the Mount Evans shelter house, a good lunch stop.

A great variety of wild flowers abound along this path in the summer and autumn. During the latter season the Beaver Meadows area is a particularly attractive one. Great stands of fragile yellow aspens line this trail for much of its length until it enters the thickly wooded higher elevation where more sturdy evergreens abound. Seasonally, any time except winter or early spring are good seasons for walking in Beaver Meadows.

11

A well-worn path leads up to Beaver Meadows.

Looking across Beaver Meadows, two shelter houses are visible in the
edge of the trees.

The easy, well-defined hiking path to Beaver Meadows is accessible
from the Denver-Evergreen area.

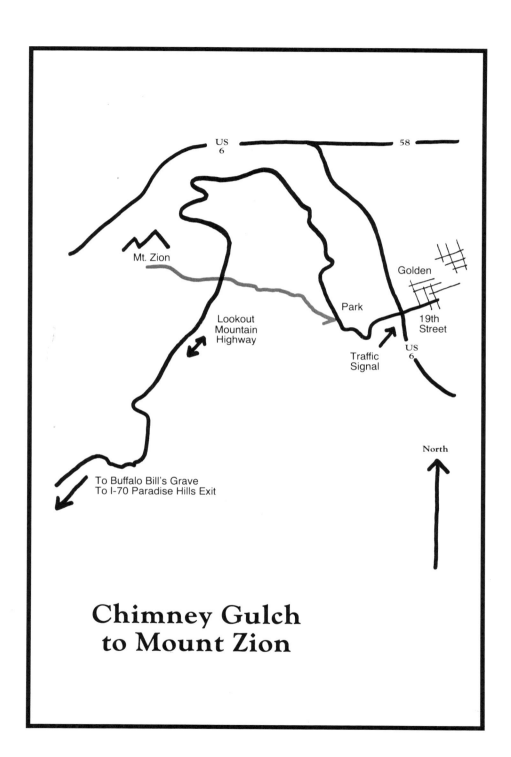

US 6

58

Mt. Zion

Golden

Park

19th Street

Lookout Mountain Highway

Traffic Signal

US 6

To Buffalo Bill's Grave
To I-70 Paradise Hills Exit

North

Chimney Gulch
to Mount Zion

CHIMNEY GULCH to
MOUNT ZION

Here is a rather short, easy hike that is virtually in the back yard of the Denver metropolitan area. On those days when the desire to hike is strong but time is short, or when the weather has not cooperated, Chimney Gulch is a fine little "ace in the hole." In the last century the Chimney Gulch Trail was a pioneer wagon route, built and operated as a toll road between Golden and Lookout Mountain. Originally, both the toll gate and the toll collector's house were located at the bottom of the gulch, close to the point where today's hiking path begins. When a fire destroyed these landmarks, only the stone chimney of the house was left standing. Hence the name became Chimney Gulch.

Begin this hike in Golden on 19th Street. Follow the street uphill to the west, cross US 6 with the light, continuing on to the point where 19th Street bends to the left. There it becomes the Lookout Mountain Highway. At the twin stone pillars the road "hairpins" abruptly to the right and passes the last of the area's homes. Now the road bends left, passing under a major group of power lines. At this point there is a turnout on the left with space for three or four cars. Pull in and park here. This is the mouth of the gulch. The old toll gate stood very close to this point.

Two trails head upward from this parking area. The one that goes straight ahead is quite steep. The other begins at the right of the parking space, goes up more to the north, and is somewhat more gradual. It is also the original stagecoach grade. A profusion of low-lying plants lines the path. Because of the rather modest altitude, most of the plants are Spanish Bayonet, wild holly, and other like vegetation. In fact, these shrubs are in the process of overgrowing the old path. As old trails of this region go this has never been a particularly well-known one, and its rather narrow right-of-way belies this lack of traffic.

Further up, the wreckage of several cars that failed to anticipate the sharp turns on the higher Lookout Mountain Highway can be seen below the trail. Near the head of the gulch the path twists up through a pretty grove of cottonwood trees and passes beside a large outcropping of native rock.

Another quarter of a mile will take you to a junction with the Lookout Mountain Highway at Windy Gap. The hill to the right or north is Mount Zion. Walk up it along the badly eroded ruts leading to the summit. There is a small but crude fireplace at the top where one may cook lunch and you'll find plenty of things to sit down on while you eat. For a view, Golden is just below you while Denver and the plains are visible to the east. Turning toward the west you can see Squaw Mountain and the tip of Mount Evans. When you are ready, return to your car by the same route.

All things considered, this is rather an easy hike. The round trip distance is less than five miles with a mere 1,000 feet of elevation gain. Because of the generally low altitude, summer hikes will be on the warm side. Late spring and autumn are the more comfortable seasons for walking in Chimney Gulch.

Table Mountain and the city of Golden can be seen from a point on
the historic Chimney Gulch Trail.

This early picture shows the last stage that climbed up Lookout
Mountain on the Chimney Gulch Trail.
Collection of Freda and Francis Rizzari

17

Coyote, Elk and Raccoon Trails

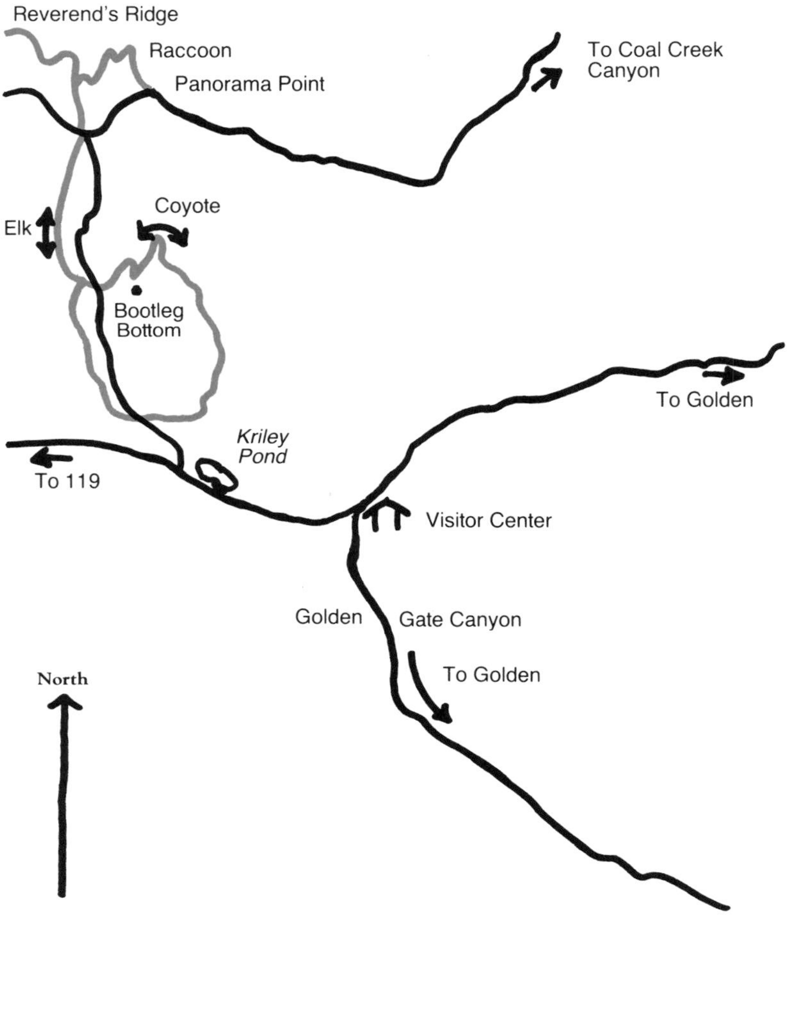

Reverend's Ridge

Raccoon

Panorama Point

To Coal Creek Canyon

Coyote

Elk

Bootleg Bottom

To Golden

Kriley Pond

To 119

Visitor Center

Golden Gate Canyon

To Golden

North

COYOTE, ELK, and RACCOON TRAILS

This is another of the pleasant but short hikes found within the Golden Gate Canyon State Park. To reach the trailhead, drive north from the Visitor's Center on the road that passes Kriley Pond. At the next junction turn right onto Mountain Base Road. Park at the first parking area, cross the road to the west and begin walking on Elk Trail. If you prefer or if pressure of time makes it expedient, continue driving north to the Bootleg Bottom trailhead. There are two parking areas here. Leave your car in the second one and cross the road to the west. At this point you pick up Coyote Trail. It runs downhill for a distance, crosses a log bridge over a little creek before starting a brief climb upward. Now the path intersects Elk Trail in an open meadow.

Now turn right or north and hike along the well-marked path paralleling Mountain Base Road. At times you are very close to this highway, but in general this is a pleasant, forested trail. Where the path crosses the paved road, continue on directly north and you will soon pick up the Elk Trail markers again. Here you will follow what appears to have been a double-rutted road. Continue to follow the old wagon ruts downhill to the marked junction with Raccoon Trail. Now turn right or east and follow the climbing switchbacks uphill to the Panorama Point overlook. Since there is now an ungraded road leading up here from Mountain Base Road, you could find other people and a few cars at this point.

The overlook itself is an ingeniously constructed shelter with wooden walks and benches. There are three dimensional profiles to aid you in identifying the handsome and rugged peaks of the Continental Divide on the western horizon. There are three of these profiles. At

A section of the Coyote, Elk, and Raccoon Trail is in Golden Gate
State Park.

From the end of the Coyote, Elk, and Raccoon Trail, one may enjoy a
panorama of the Continental Divide and the Devils Thumb.

this writing one of them incorrectly identifies Parrys Peak as Party Peak. Otherwise they are fine and provide a helpful perspective to the person interested in mountain identification. There is a durable sanitary facility here too, constructed of brick. If your sense of humor runs in this vein, certain obvious comparisons may be drawn between this structure and the human female anatomy, if appropriate.

Time permitting, take the brief but pretty trail over to Reverend's Ridge. If not, go back by the same route and return to your car. If time is short, walk down the auto road instead. Although less interesting, it intersects rather quickly at the point where you crossed the road on the way up. From here it is downhill nearly all the way back to the Bootleg Bottom parking area. Round trip mileage for this hike will depend on the variations you may choose, but will average in the neighborhood of five miles. From late April through summer and into late autumn are the preferred seasons for this easy walk. We have occasionally been able to enjoy this hike in mid-November without discomfort. When the aspens don their mantle of yellow gold, this is a truly lovely place.

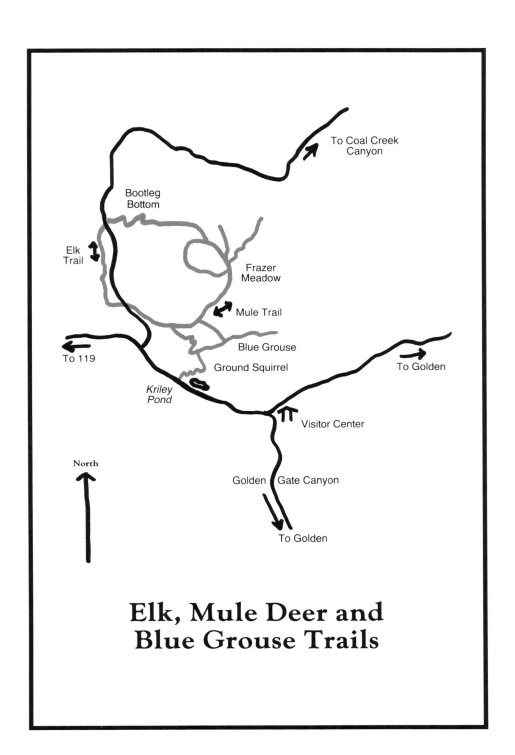

To Coal Creek Canyon

Bootleg Bottom

Elk Trail

Frazer Meadow

Mule Trail

Blue Grouse

To 119

Ground Squirrel

Kriley Pond

To Golden

Visitor Center

North

Golden Gate Canyon

To Golden

Elk, Mule Deer and Blue Grouse Trails

ELK, MULE DEER, and
BLUE GROUSE TRAILS

This is a circle trip within Golden Gate Canyon State Park. It can be started from either the Kriley Pond trailhead or from the one immediately to the north, below Bootleg Bottom. We prefer the latter, mostly because it allows a slightly longer hike through very pretty terrain. Begin on Elk Trail and stay with it all the way to Frazer Meadow.

If you choose the somewhat shorter route start at the Kriley Pond parking loop and follow Ground Squirrel and Mule Deer Trails to Frazer Meadow. Do not take the right fork at the intersection with Blue Grouse Trail. It is steep from this end. These are well-landscaped paths, easy to follow, and well-marked. They wander in and out through evergreen and deciduous aspen trees, gaining altitude gradually. There are good views of James Peak, the Continental Divide, Mt. Evans, and Squaw Mountain as you walk along.

Just fifty yards or so before you cross the foot bridge to the old buildings in Frazer Meadow there is an interesting side trip you might enjoy, but the trail is hard to find. Watch for a trampled grass path leaving the established trail and running left or northwest into a sparse aspen grove. Although many people know of this digression, unless one of them has walked it in the past few days it is not visible and you probably should forget it. It leads to a well-worn path not shown on Visitor's Center maps. In places this trail becomes an obviously old double rutted wagon road. In late June the columbine and other wild flowers are abundant here and are well worth the side trip.

We leave this trail after a half mile, cutting abruptly off through very dense undergrowth and bearing to your right. In the absence of any trail you must "bushwhack" across several sticky little stream crossings. When you reach the rocky hill turn sharply right again and walk south, then west across a clearing to intersect Coyote Trail. Turn right again and return to Frazer Meadow for a lunch stop.

After eating, begin your return on Mule Deer Trail. Where it intersects with Ground Squirrel Trail go left for a short distance on Ground Squirrel to Blue Grouse Trail. Turn right again and follow this latter path back to your car. One unmarked path goes off to the left and should be avoided.

Since this pretty circle walk involves several different trails, a copy of the free map from the Visitor's Center should be consulted before you start. Except for the side trip near Frazer Meadow all of the other trails are shown. On second thought, unless you have a pretty good sense of direction, avoid the side trip. The entire round trip involves about five miles of easy walking. Summer or autumn would be the preferred season.

Some hikers walk along the Elk, Mule Deer, and Blue Grouse Trail.

This sylvan scene is a typical one along the Elk, Mule Deer, and Blue
Grouse Trail.

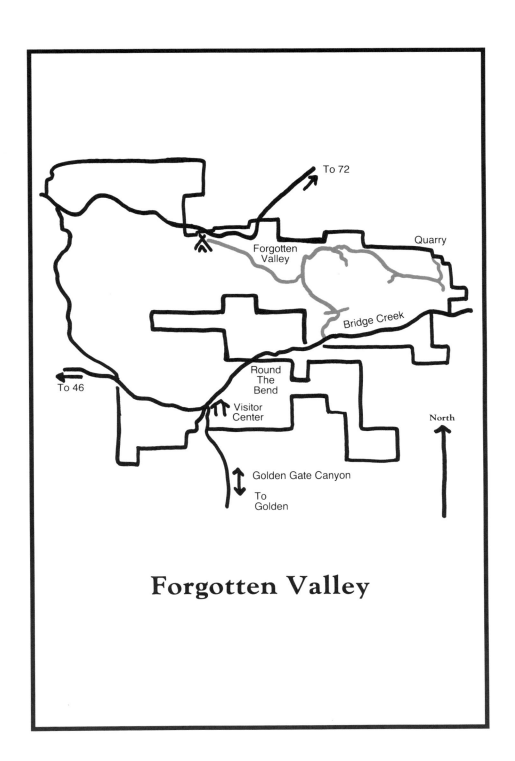

To 72

Quarry

Forgotten
Valley

Bridge Creek

To 46

Round
The
Bend

Visitor
Center

North

Golden Gate Canyon

To
Golden

Forgotten Valley

FORGOTTEN VALLEY

Here is a short but rather pretty hike that is close to the metropolitan area. It lies within the Golden Gate Canyon State Park, fifteen miles northwest of the city of Golden. Hikers can reach the park most easily from Denver by following 6th Avenue west to the city of Golden. Turn right at the junction with Highway 58, then north on Highway 93 to the winding Golden Gate Canyon Road. Turn left into the canyon and drive fourteen miles to the park. Boulder hikers can take Highway 93 south to the edge of Golden, then right into the canyon and proceed as previously described.

Incidentally, the open meadow southwest of the junction of 93 with the Golden Gate road was the site of Golden Gate City, an 1859 mining supply town. It was abandoned when a better road was built through nearby Clear Creek Canyon. Most of the residents gave it up and migrated down into Golden.

As you enter the park, turn right to the Visitor's Center, pay the small entrance fee, then drive northwest past Round the Bend picnic area. Continuing on, the road briefly crosses private property and re-enters the park. At Bridge Creek, on your left, there is a small parking area adjacent to the start of Burro Trail. Follow the path across a creek and up the wooded valley to the junction with Buffalo Trail.

Now take Buffalo Trail to the left and continue hiking uphill to the northwest, passing the junction of Eagle Trail. Now the country becomes more open and the path shows signs of having been a double rut wagon road at some time in the past. Some cactus and a variety of pretty wild flowers border the path. Like all floral displays, this one changes with the seasons, altitude, and rainfall.

Forgotten Valley in the Golden Gate Canyon State Park has an
easy-to-follow trail.

An abandoned homestead and reservoir are located near the head of
Forgotten Valley.

Directly ahead you will see a group of abandoned structures. This is Hidden Valley. The presence of a small reservoir probably means that this was someone's homestead. A barn and several log structures stand beyond the reservoir. From time to time we have seen people fishing here. It may or may not be stocked.

There is an additional split in the trail at this point. The left fork continues northwest, terminating at Rifleman Phillips campground. The right fork twists upward around the shoulder of Windy Peak, ending at a point called Quarry. When you have reached the Forgotten Valley structures, you will have walked just under two miles. If you choose to go on to the Rifleman Phillips facility, the total distance will be slightly more than three miles. If you go on around Windy Peak to Quarry, the total distance is five and a half miles.

Since Golden Gate Park's altitude is relatively low, summer days can become a bit warm for extended walking. For this reason we prefer late spring or early autumn for this hike. Incidentally, Golden Gate Park now contains more than fifty miles of maintained hiking paths. All are clearly shown on the free map that is obtainable at the Visitor's Center.

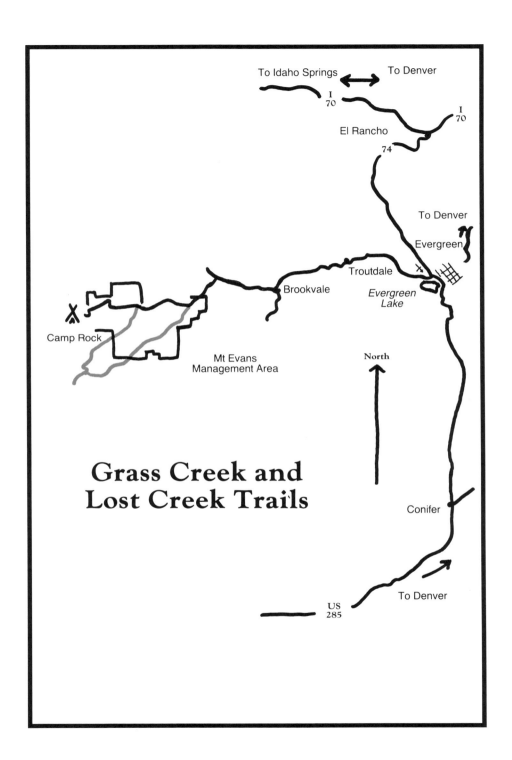

To Idaho Springs ⟷ To Denver

I 70

I 70

El Rancho

74

To Denver

Evergreen

Troutdale

Brookvale

Evergreen Lake

Camp Rock

Mt Evans Management Area

North

Grass Creek and Lost Creek Trails

Conifer

To Denver

US 285

GRASS CREEK and
LOST CREEK TRAILS

In recent years a whole series of relatively new hiking paths have been opened up in the general area contiguous to the town of Evergreen. Some of the trails are quite old, others were wagon roads used by homesteaders, but a growing number are newly established solely as foot paths. All are administered by the Arapaho National Forest. Most are quite scenic, a few are of historical interest, and all have the virtue of being close to the metropolitan area.

Since this particular hike takes you within the Mount Evans Elk Management Area and because these temperamental but beautiful animals thrive best on seasonal privacy, one may hike this trail only between June 15th and the Labor Day weekend. Otherwise, except during hunting season, the area is closed to all traffic.

To begin this hike, drive out of Evergreen on Colorado State Highway 74 to the Upper Bear Creek Road. Follow this road for about six miles to the junction. Here you should turn right and follow the Singing River Ranch signs for a couple of miles to a second junction. Turn left now and continue along the graded road to the Mount Evans Elk Management headquarters building. Parking for several cars and public rest rooms are available here. From the parking area go to the left around the gate and begin walking uphill along the old original road. You are now on the Grass Creek Trail. Continue walking along this road-trail to Groundhog Flat where a tall chimney, a foundation and some fencing remain from homesteading days. Leave the road at this point and walk to your right across the meadow.

The big peaks ahead of you are Mount Evans, Mount Epaulet, and Mount Rosalie. Follow this trail as it leads

The Grass Creek and Lost Creek Trail passes the chimney and fireplace of an abandoned homestead.

From a point near the summit of the Grass Creek Trail, Mount Evans and the Continental Divide are seen.

generally downhill for just over a half mile to the junction with the Lost Creek Trail.

At the Lost Creek sign, turn right once more and walk approximately one additional mile, generally uphill through towering aspen groves. At the top of the final long incline the path ends at the graded Camp Rock Road. Go to the right at the signs and walk downhill, back to your car. The total walking distance for this circle trip is between five and six miles.

The seasonal limitations for the Grass Creek and Lost Creek Trails have already been noted. Actually, summer is the best season for this trek, although autumn would be nice. Not only is this an easy, mostly shady hike, but it offers the opportunity to observe the Mount Evans elk herd under relatively natural conditions. Perhaps you will see them, but perhaps not. But carry a camera anyway.

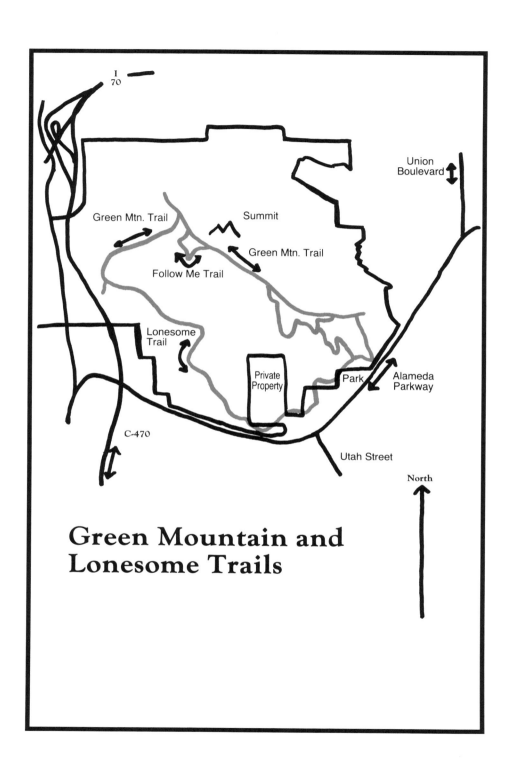

Green Mountain and Lonesome Trails

GREEN MOUNTAIN and LONESOME TRAILS

Green Mountain is one of the newer trails systems that were established as a part of the Jefferson County Open Space program. It has the dual advantage of being at the edge of the metropolitan area and of being low enough in elevation to be accessible for most of the year. It has two trailheads, each is well marked, and they lie about a mile apart. We prefer to begin at the more easterly one.

To reach the trail, drive out West Alameda Avenue toward the foothills from Denver. Continue on past the traffic light at Union Boulevard and park on the north side where Utah Avenue ends at West Alameda. Here you will find ample parking for about a dozen cars, and a small metal box on a post containing maps of the entire Green Mountain group of trails.

A short distance up the path from the trailhead the route divides. We prefer to go left or west at this point, following the Lonesome Trail to the main trailhead for the park. Along the way you may enjoy a good view of the Red Rocks amphitheatre and of the Alameda Hog Back road. Where the trail crosses an access road, continue straight ahead and up the hill. As you drop down again, the main parking area is ahead of you. Here the Lonesome Trail ends.

At this point you pick up the Green Mountain Trail. It climbs slightly past a couple of weirdly shaped rocks. The second one resembles a seal. We call it the "Great Seal of the United States." Now the trail becomes a crude road and climbs steeply to the summit of Green Mountain. At the next junction keep to your right, but stay on the main Green Mountain Trail. The John Hayden Trail leads down to Interstate 70, and the short

The well-marked Green Mountain Trail.

From the top of the Green Mountain Trail, one view looks toward the east, with downtown Denver in the distance.

Follow Me Trail contours around a little hill to a pleasing viewpoint.

Continue walking generally southeast past the turnoff to the radio tower. Here you may enjoy a panorama of the Front Range from Pikes Peak north to Longs and beyond. Far below you, Golden and Denver are fully visible. Incidentally, this is a fine lunch stop. From this point the trail is downhill all the way to the point where you left your car. Merely stay on the main Green Mountain Trail.

In all, the total elevation gain is just under 1,000 feet and the walking distance is barely over six miles. We prefer autumn as the best time for this hike. In spring the path can be soggy, and summer days can become a bit tepid at this low altitude. Early winter can be pleasant on Green Mountain. We have walked this path comfortably in December if it is barren of snow. But with only minor limitations, this is a year round trail.

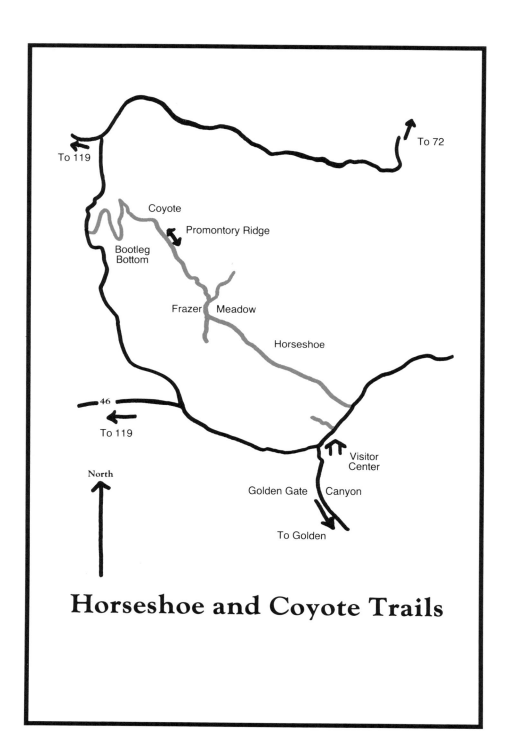

To 72

To 119

Coyote

Promontory Ridge

Bootleg
Bottom

Frazer Meadow

Horseshoe

46

To 119

North

Visitor
Center

Golden Gate Canyon

To Golden

Horseshoe and Coyote Trails

HORSESHOE and COYOTE TRAILS

In common with the preceding chapters in this section, both of these trails are part of the Golden Gate Canyon State Park. Drive northwest for fifteen miles up that canyon from Golden to the park headquarters. Here you should register, pay the fee, and pick up a copy of the map showing the trails. Now drive northeast up Ralston Gulch past the Black Bear trailhead to the Horseshoe Trail parking area, which will be on your left. Leave the car here and begin walking up the well-marked Horseshoe Trail.

This path gains its elevation gradually, climbing up from 8,200 feet to 9,000 feet in just over two miles. In places this route shows the unmistakable scars of having once been a wagon road. Looking off to the right you will see the rock cribbing that once secured the road to the steep hillside. Horseshoe Trail enters Frazer Meadow from the southeast. Here you must follow Mule Deer Trail for a few yards to the junction with Coyote Trail.

Go left at this point on Coyote Trail and follow it through alternate areas of open clearing and thick groves of aspen and evergreen trees. Walk about two and a half miles more to the summit of Promontory Ridge. Here among the rocks you will find a fine sheltered picnic area. Here you may enjoy an attractive view of the front range from Mt. Evans on the south to Longs Peak on the north. The highway below you is Mountain Base Road, and the parking area is the trailhead for Bootleg Bottom.

If you have made prior arrangements for someone to meet you, hike down the hill to the parking area just mentioned. If not, return to your car at the Horseshoe trailhead by the same route, enjoying the vistas that were behind you on the way up. Best seasons for this walk are summer and autumn. Due to the abundant growth of aspen trees, late September is a particularly attractive time for this hike. The total distance, round trip as described, is about five miles.

Much of the Horseshoe and Coyote Trail wanders through low-growing vegetation.

The Continental Divide and South Arapaho Peak are seen from the end of the Horseshoe and Coyote Trail. Arapaho Pass is at center.

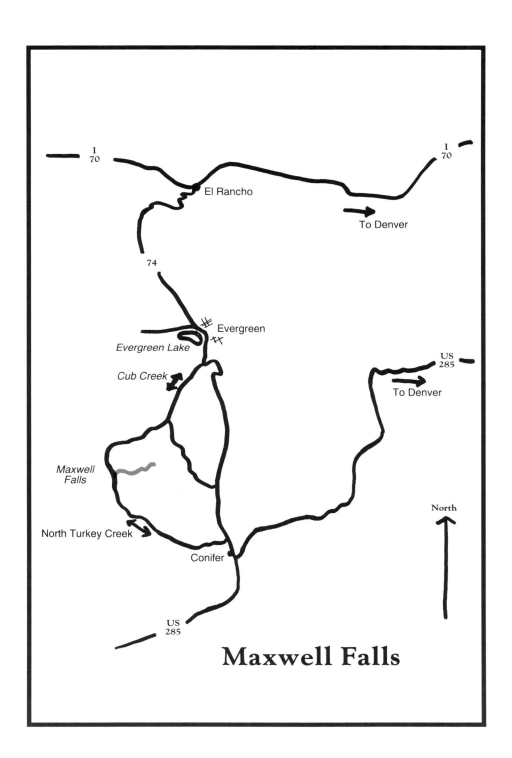

Maxwell Falls

MAXWELL FALLS

Of all the hikes in this book, this one to Maxwell Falls is easily the least strenuous. If this criteria appeals to you, drive south from Evergreen on the road toward Conifer, turning right at the Beaver Brook sign. Follow the signs all the way to Beaver Brook Lodge. Beyond the lodge the road forks. Keep to the left, actually straight ahead, at this junction and continue on to the marked Maxwell Falls trailhead. Both the sign and the parking area are on the left, just below the road.

The Maxwell Falls Trail is a broad path, easy to follow. Although there are a number of less obvious side trails, stay on the main path. All of the side trails eventually return to the main trail. Since the right of way follows the creek, stay within hearing range and you can't go wrong. In general the trail is downhill for the first half mile.

Actually, Maxwell Falls is not more than a mile from the trailhead. You will hear it before you see it, on your right below the path. There are two separate falls here. One is fairly tall and thin while the second is hardly more than a series of rapids.

Since the distance walked to this point is minimal, continue on past the falls on the same trail. The path crosses two open meadows before descending to the stream. Here the route follows the watercourse through to the same graded road that you followed from the lodge to the trailhead.

At this point you may choose to retrace your steps, returning to your car by the same route. Obviously the other alternative is to turn left here and walk back along the road.

Maxwell Falls is open to hiking from late spring through the last of autumn. Although this trail offers

There are rocky sections along the Maxwell Falls Trail.

This is one of the cascades at Maxwell Falls.

little along the line of exciting mountain scenery, it does offer a shaded, protected trail affording a short, leisurely walk in the foothills.

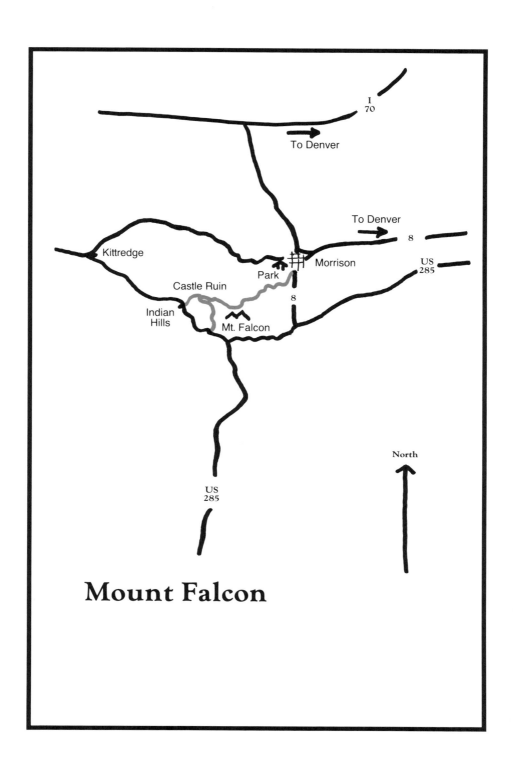

Mount Falcon

MOUNT FALCON

At the present time there are three different trails that lead one to Mount Falcon. The first is only a mile long, each way; the other two are longer. The shorter one leaves a marked trailhead on Colorado Highway 74, the Indian Hills road which connects US 285 with the town of Kittredge. The second begins at the water tower in the town of Morrison and proceeds steeply up a ravine to meet the old original wagon road. The third route is the original and is slightly longer but is by far the most interesting and historic. To hike this trail, drive through Morrison toward US 285. At the metal Highway Department building on the right, turn west or uphill to the right. At the end of this graded street, turn right and park by the marked trailhead.

John Brisben Walker was the founder of Cosmopolitan Magazine and was the man who sold the Red Rocks Park area to the city of Denver. Walker built a summer home on the summit of Mount Falcon. Later he dreamed of a summer White House for the President of the United States, adjacent to his own mansion of course. The trail up here from Morrison was his original wagon road, narrower now and overgrown in places, but a pleasant foot path for today's hiker. Some years ago Jefferson County acquired this tract of land, did some work on the trail and made it available for public use.

For openers, the path starts up the rounded shoulder of a low hill to the west of Morrison. Typically, it follows a series of switchbacks, gaining altitude gradually as it makes its way up among low-growing deciduous bushes. Higher up a growth of modest-size evergreens line the trail. Where intersections occur, markers have been placed or logs have been laid across wrong turns. When you reach the ridge summit and can see the Front

Range to the west you are within a mile of the castle. As you continue along the path, wider here, the castle will be to your right, nestled in among the trees.

Because the structure was burned early in the present century, the upper story and roof are entirely gone. Thirty-five years ago more of the outside and bearing walls were standing than one sees at present, but there is still a great deal to be enjoyed. Sturdy wooden fences have been installed to minimize the wear and tear associated with public access. When you walk over to the edge of the ruin, Mount Morrison and the Red Rocks amphitheatre are visible.

If you continue to the west along the trail you followed up here it will take you out of the trees and across an open meadow into another growth of evergreens. Follow the trail markers up into the trees to reach a smaller structure, allegedly built as a study for the President. On the patio there used to be a marble slab that carried the inscription proclaiming this as a "Summer White House, a gift of the people of Colorado, 1911." In recent years the plaque was moved to the site of the home for Presidents that was never completed. To see it follow the signs directing you to "Walker's Dream."

Curiously, no President ever visited the site. William Howard Taft accepted an invitation but never came, although he visited other places in Colorado. Woodrow Wilson also accepted an invitation, but got only as far as Denver. Rumors persist that Calvin Coolidge once visited the castle, but they are untrue.

From the alleged study there is a path that passes beside a rather picturesque old well that is adorned with an inscription in German. Translated, it means "At the Well in Front of the Gate," a favorite early church hymn. The path goes on up to a large wooden observation platform called the "Crow's Nest."

From Morrison, the round trip distance for this hike is six miles. Although we have made this trek during all four seasons, summer and autumn are the best choices.

The roofless ruins of the Walker castle are now protected by the
Jefferson County Open Space Department.

From a point near Walker's castle, one may enjoy this view
to the west.

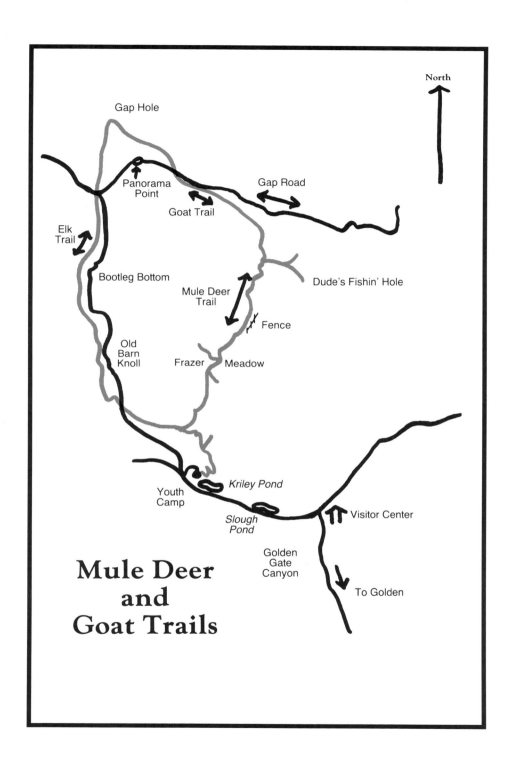

North

Gap Hole

Panorama
Point

Goat Trail

Gap Road

Elk
Trail

Bootleg Bottom

Mule Deer
Trail

Dude's Fishin' Hole

Fence

Old
Barn
Knoll

Frazer   Meadow

Kriley Pond

Youth
Camp

Slough
Pond

Visitor Center

Golden
Gate
Canyon

To Golden

Mule Deer
and
Goat Trails

MULE DEER and
GOAT TRAILS

Golden Gate Canyon State Park is one of our newer recreation areas. Historically, Golden Gate Canyon was one of the most used migrant routes to the mountains in 1859–60. Eager gold seekers thronged up to the Black Hawk–Central City areas from Golden Gate City by way of this early trail. At a later time homesteaders migrated into the region and some of the cribbed wagon roads established by them are used as hiking trails within the park today. Something in excess of 8,500 acres of wooded hillsides, paths, open meadows, and watercourses are included within the park. The altitude here ranges from 7,600 to 10,400 feet.

To reach the park, drive fifteen miles up the canyon northwest from Golden on Colorado State Highway 46. Stop at park headquarters and pay the modest entrance fee, currently one dollar per day or five dollars for the season. While you are there, pick up one of the free maps of the trails, then continue up on the road toward Central City. Go on past Slough Pond and Youth Camp to Mountain Base Road. Turn right here, then immediately right again to the parking area.

Walk uphill past the brick sanitary facility. Here hikers can give full rein to their imaginations and make the usual remarks about such structures when built from this material. As you enter the trees, the path swings abruptly toward the northwest and negotiates a couple of switchbacks. Approximately a quarter of a mile further along, the Blue Grouse Trail takes off to the right. Keep left here and follow the Mule Deer markers. At this point you will also find signs for the Ground Squirrel Trail, which uses this same route for a short distance.

Go right at the next place where the trail splits, in this

On the Mule Deer and Goat Trail, we pass the old homestead structures in Frazer Meadows.

Longs Peak is visible from the highest place on the Mule Deer and Goat Trail.

case on the point of a switchback. Now continue up to an open area formerly known as Blackman Meadow where an early black pioneer homesteaded. At the writing two of his buildings still stand. For some reason the name has now been changed to Frazer Meadow. Cross this area and walk uphill toward the north. Keep right where the next division of the trail occurs. Coyote Trail leaves the path toward the northwest from here.

Now pretty mountain panoramas begin to be visible. If you look back to the rear as you climb, James Peak, on the Continental Divide, comes into view. A bit further along, on a switchback to the left, Squaw and Chief Mountains are briefly visible. Then as you approach the top of the 9,200 foot ridge, Mount Evans and Rogers Peak can be seen off to the west.

From this point the trail runs downhill for about a mile, briefly paralleling a wire fence that separates the park from private land holdings. Near the foot of the hill a side trail runs off to the right for a long quarter of a mile to a pond called Dude's Fishin' Hole.

From this intersection the main trail continues on to the northwest through heavily forested terrain, crosses the Gap Road and continues on up to Panorama Point. Stop here and enjoy a 100-mile panorama of the Continental Divide. Now return to the Gap Road crossing and follow two miles of Goat Trail to Gap Hole, then 1.3 miles of Raccoon Trail to the Information Center. Walk south now on Elk Trail, past Bootleg Bottom and Old Barn Knoll to the parking area where you left the car.

The total walking distance for this hike is just over twelve miles. This can be halved by asking a patient friend to meet you at the Gap Road intersection near Panorama Point. Best seasons for this hike are summer and autumn, although we have covered much of it in February, depending on snow conditions.

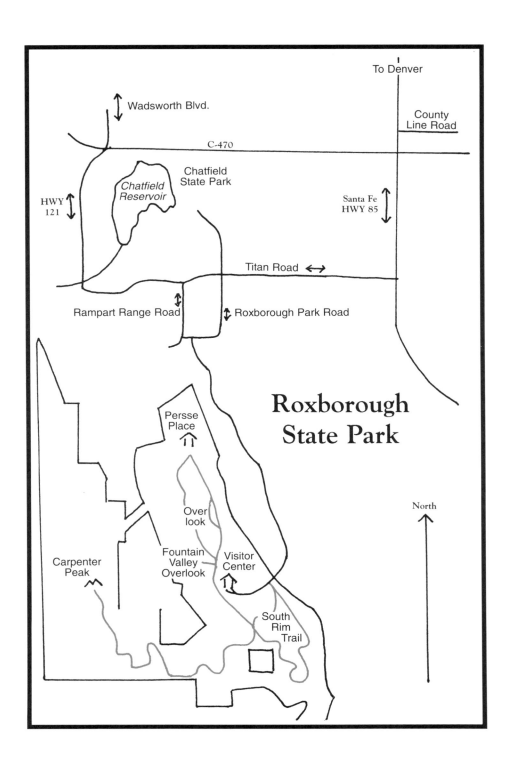

To Denver

County Line Road

Wadsworth Blvd.

C-470

Chatfield State Park

Chatfield Reservoir

HWY 121

Santa Fe HWY 85

Titan Road ↔

Rampart Range Road

Roxborough Park Road

Persse Place

Roxborough State Park

Over look

North

Carpenter Peak

Fountain Valley Overlook

Visitor Center

South Rim Trail

ROXBOROUGH STATE PARK

In this book's first edition the heading for this chapter was Roxborough Park. Since that time many changes have occurred, suggesting that this chapter and its map should be revised. Incidentally, there is still a Roxborough Park, but it is now a housing development. The state of Colorado began acquiring land in this area in the 1970s for a state park. Although people were allowed to enter Roxborough, it was by permit only until water and sanitary facilities were acquired in 1987. After that date it was officially opened to visitors as Roxborough State Park. The state park occupies a much more limited acreage.

The Roxborough State Park encompasses a southerly continuation of the colorful sandstone escarpments that surface along the eastern slope of the Dakota Hogback. The Garden of the Gods, near Colorado Springs, contains other examples of the same formations. West of Denver the Red Rocks Park and Amphitheater are possibly the best known examples of these Fountain formations. Denver acquired its Red Rocks Park from John Brisben Walker, founder of *Cosmopolitan* magazine.

Roxborough State Park consists of many additional Fountain formations: huge slabs of salmon pink, dark orange, and brick red sandstone monoliths that were forced up out of the earth's crust in prehistoric times. Some tower 200 or more feet high. Around their bases a low, dense undergrowth of scrub oak, Ponderosa Pine, and Douglas Fir trees enhance the region's natural beauty. Following a rain, the color saturation becomes intense.

On earlier visits to Roxborough we were able to hike south of the present state park boundaries on a double-rutted trail that entered Pike National Forest. Originally, this was a small section of a nineteenth century stagecoach route that bisected the Roxborough area, providing connections between the towns of South Platte, West Creek, Woodland Park, Divide, and Cripple Creek. An 1895 Gazatteer lists the Spotswood and McClellan coach line as the likely operators. This historic old trail is now filled with homes and is outside the state park boundaries. It is closed to the public and no access is permitted.

Within Roxborough State Park the early Henry Persse (or Purce) homestead still stands near the park's north end. Current plans call for the preservation and restoration of the still-standing structures, as park budgets permit. The assumption that the homestead was once a stagecoach stop are incorrect.

To visit Roxborough State Park from Denver, drive south on Colorado Highway 121, which is South Wadsworth Boulevard, until it turns south past the Chatfield State Recreation area. Continue south on 121 to the Waterton Road, just before the entrance to Martin-Marietta. Turn left or east on the Waterton Road to North Rampart Range Road, then turn south past Roxborough Village and the Foothills Water Treatment Plant. At the junction of Rampart Range Road and Roxborough Park Road, turn briefly left, then right onto the state park access road.

An alternate route follows U.S. Highway 85, South Santa Fe, to Titan Road. Turn right or west on Titan Road, which curves to the south to become North Rampart Range Road. Continue driving south past Roxborough Village and the Foothills Water Treatment Plant. Turn left onto Roxborough Park Road and go about fifty yards to the park entrance. Be sure to obtain a pass and one of the attractive brochures. Five hikes are shown on the park map. Their mileages vary from 1.25 to 3 miles. They are classified from gentle to moderate-steep.

Since Roxborough State Park is located at a fairly low elevation, summer's cooler days are preferred for walking. Late spring and autumn are our favorite seasons for hiking here.

Roxborough Park has stately formations of sandstone.

Henry Purce homesteaded in Roxborough Park.

57

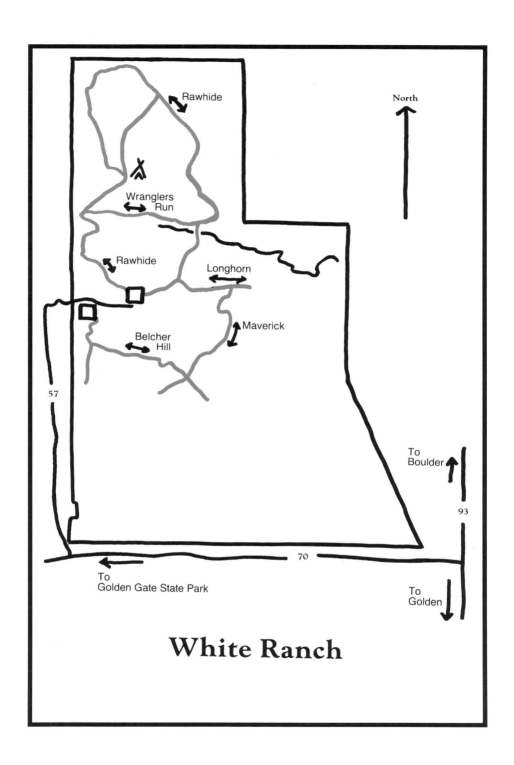

Rawhide

North

Wranglers
Run

Rawhide

Longhorn

Maverick

Belcher
Hill

57

To
Boulder

93

70

To
Golden Gate State Park

To
Golden

White Ranch

WHITE RANCH

Until fairly recent times this area was an honest-to-goodness working ranch, an extensive spread located high in the foothills west of Golden. Currently a portion of it has become a part of the Jefferson County Open Space program. It is open to all for recreational purposes.

To reach White Ranch take Highway 93 north out of Golden for a half mile to County Road 70, the Golden Gate Canyon Road. Turn left here and drive slightly more than four miles to County Road 57 where you will see a directional sign for White Ranch. Turn right at this point. This is the Crawford Hill or Gulch Road. It also involves just over four miles of driving until you come to another White Ranch sign. Turn right or east by the sign and proceed for one and a half miles to the second of two parking areas.

Because this is a rather dry area be sure to carry water with you. From the parking area, a path leads over to a nice picnic spot in a grove of evergreens. There are restroom facilities adjacent to the picnic tables. Now look for the sign directing you to the Rawhide Trail and turn left onto the path, walking generally north. The Rawhide Trail passes a junction with the Waterhole Trail and loops around to the south past Sourdough Springs camping area and Wrangler's Run Trail. Continue walking on the Rawhide Trail back to the parking area where you left your car.

At this point, if time permits, we like to return to the Rawhide Trail. But this time we turn east to Longhorn Trail, then south on Maverick Trail. At the next junction turn right and walk northwest on the Belcher Hill path which will take you to that first parking area on the road in from the Crawford Gulch Road. Now walk along the

Broader sections of the circular trail wind through White Ranch.

An early structure remains along the White Ranch Trail.

graded road for the short distance to your car. At this writing there are free maps at the trailhead which show this entire route.

When you have completed this hike as described you will have walked a total of about six miles, circling a generous portion of the park. The gain in elevation is only 1,000 feet, but much of the walk involves going alternately up and down over the rolling hillsides.

We are fond of White Ranch for three reasons. First, it is close to the metropolitan area and can be hiked at most any season although we prefer spring and autumn. Second, it is a wildlife refuge and no fences separate you from the deer and other animals and birds that live here. All are quite tame and we have rarely failed to see them. Unfortunately, diamondback rattlesnakes live here too and are present during warm weather. Avoid piles of rubble and large rocks as these are their likely habitats. Bears, mountain lions, and wild turkeys are also found in the White Ranch area, but in lesser numbers. Third and finally, the big picnic area adjacent to the parking lot is a gem of a place when the moon is full. It affords a marvelous view overlooking the brightly lighted Denver metropolitan area. Try it, you'll love it too.

American Indian lore is replete with tales of the coyote. Today, this highly intelligent scavenger is commonly seen throughout the mountains and even around the fringe of some Colorado cities.

Boulder County

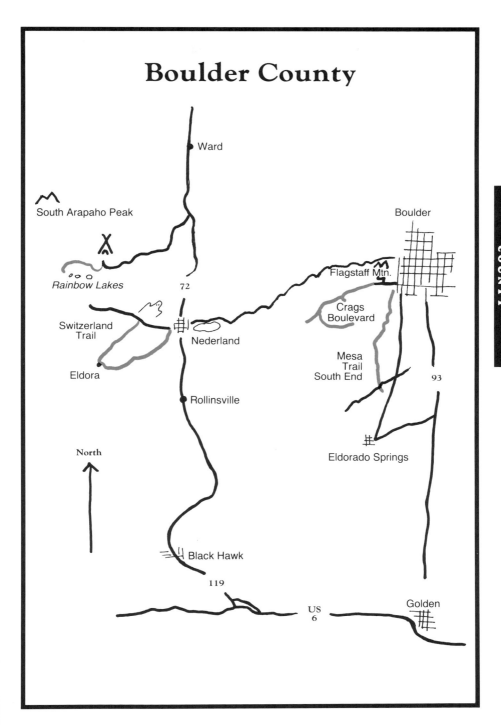

Ward

South Arapaho Peak

Rainbow Lakes

72

Boulder

Flagstaff Mtn.

Crags
Boulevard

Switzerland
Trail

Nederland

Mesa
Trail
South End

93

Eldora

Rollinsville

North

Eldorado Springs

Black Hawk

119

US
6

Golden

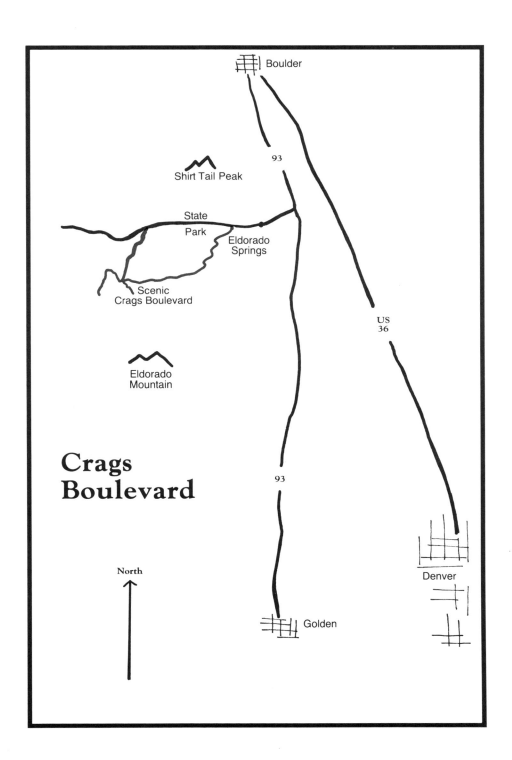

Boulder

93

Shirt Tail Peak

State
Park

Eldorado
Springs

Scenic
Crags Boulevard

US
36

Eldorado
Mountain

Crags
Boulevard

93

North

Golden

Denver

CRAGS BOULEVARD

At the turn of the present century one of Colorado's prime resorts was located in a deep canyon at Eldorado Springs in Boulder County. A large hotel and a small town grew up around the naturally heated waters. Health seekers came here from far and wide to "take the waters" for ailments that ranged from asthma to arthritis. High above the hostelry the great Ivy Baldwin regularly walked a high wire that had been stretched tautly between the sheer canyon walls above South Boulder Creek.

In 1900 a second resort hotel, very plush, was constructed on a lofty finger of land high above Eldorado Canyon. It was called the Crags. To simplify access, a two mile long twisting, serpentine road was cut into the nearly vertical face of the canyon wall. Although intended as a wagon road, it was soon adapted to accommodate early touring cars. It was known as Crags Boulevard. For those sensitive persons who shunned gas buggies, a costly funicular was built. It descended almost vertically from the posh resort down to the road that follows South Boulder Creek.

The Crags hotel was destined for a short life. It burned to the ground in 1912 and was never rebuilt. As the years passed, Crags Boulevard disintegrated with disuse. With time the vegetation closed in and the road was nearly forgotten. Today it is just a narrow hiking path. As a hike it possesses the combined virtues of being close to the metropolitan area as well as being rich in a somewhat obscure local history.

If this hike seems appealing, take Colorado Highway 93, which connects Boulder and Golden. Turn off at the Eldorado Springs sign and drive west through the town and into the newly created Eldorado Canyon State Park.

Continue along the unpaved shelf road to the marked trailhead on your left. This distance from Highway 93 to the start of your path is 3.8 miles. At this point you will find adequate parking for a half dozen or so cars.

Two trails begin here. Both run generally south and come together a mile or so up the canyon. The one to the left was the original wagon road while the other is a shorter but steeper foot path. At the point where the two trails merge a huge concrete pipe can be seen. It belongs to the Denver Water Board and was built to carry water through three ranges from the Western Slope by way of the Moffat Tunnel to the Denver metropolitan area.

Near the water conveyer the trail bends sharply to the right, then rounds a corner to the left in another quarter mile, following the contour of the canyon wall. In general this is an easy trail, heavily wooded for its entire distance. There are pretty wild flowers growing beside the path, and several patches of poison ivy. High above, on the opposite wall of the canyon, lies the grade of the Rio Grande Railroad and one of its tunnels. This is the main line to Winter Park and the Western Slope.

Where the trail levels out the large open meadow was the site of the Crags Hotel. A depression in the ground marks the location of the elaborate fountain that formerly graced the hotel grounds. Over at the edge, where one looks down into the canyon, a portion of the funicular loading platform can be seen along with the scar where it descended into the canyon.

If you choose to continue along the path beyond the hotel site it will take you to Inspiration Point, a favorite view spot during resort days. Either this or the hotel site are fine for lunch stops. You have now walked about two and a half miles. On your return why not take the other trail from the water pipe, just for variety? When you reach your car the total distance traveled will be approximately five miles.

The preferred seasons for this pleasant trek would be late spring, summer, or autumn. Since there are several groves of aspen trees along the right-of-way the autumn time would be our preference.

Evelyn Brown hikes along a section of the old trail up to the site of
the Crags Hotel.

In this early view we see the several structures of the old Crags Hotel.
Crags Boulevard shows at the lower right.

Collection of Helen Kneale

Gregory Canyon and Saddle Rock

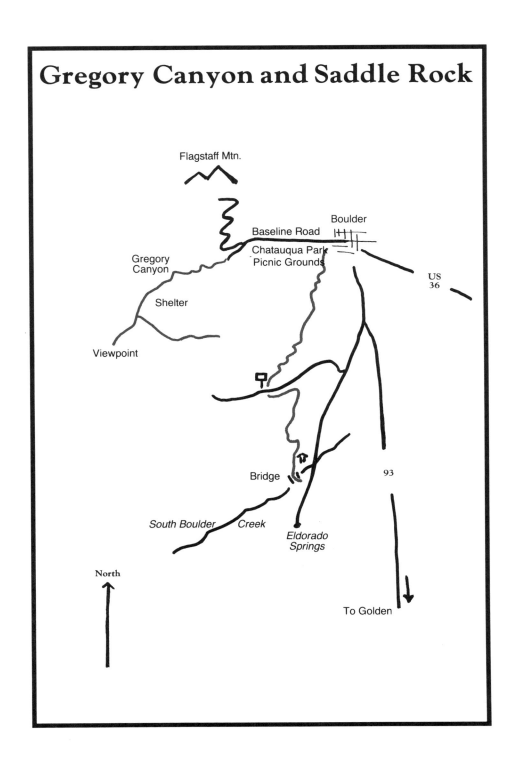

Flagstaff Mtn.

Baseline Road

Boulder

Gregory
Canyon

Chatauqua Park
Picnic Grounds

US
36

Shelter

Viewpoint

Bridge

93

South Boulder   Creek

Eldorado
Springs

North

To Golden

GREGORY CANYON and SADDLE ROCK

This is a short, easy hike to a pretty place that is also close to the metropolitan area. Among Colorado's front range communities, Boulder has taken the lead in surrounding itself with a green belt that has been set aside for recreational purposes. This hike is within the Boulder Mountain Park system.

If you are coming from outside of Boulder, take the Turnpike, US 36, to the Baseline Road exit. Baseline is a surveying term and is used here because the Baseline Road is actually the 40th parallel. Townships north of it are designated as Township 1, north, etc.; and south as Township 1, south, and so on. Originally the 40th parallel divided what is now Colorado between Kansas and Nebraska. At that time Boulder was in Nebraska and Denver was in Kansas. The 40th parallel continued all the way to the crest of the Continental Divide.

Follow the Baseline Road west through Boulder. Turn left on the graded road where Baseline turns right to ascend Flagstaff Mountain. Follow the graded road to the picnic ground and park on the circle drive. Gregory Canyon begins here and runs generally west for a generous half mile where it bends to the southwest for an additional half mile to a county-owned shelter.

Now take the Green Mountain Trail southeast to Saddle Rock Trail and follow it back to the northeast. Climb up onto Saddle Rock when you reach it and enjoy the view as you eat your lunch. We have often watched hang gliders from this vantage point. They fly off the side of Flagstaff Mountain, circle about and land in one of the open areas on the western fringe of the city.

This trail lies primarily in shade, is very well laid out, and both gains and loses a lot of altitude along the way.

Looking toward the west from the top of the Gregory Canyon Trail
we get this panorama of the Continental Divide.

From the end of the Gregory Canyon Trail the view looks out across
the city of Boulder.

The round trip walking distance is in the neighborhood of five miles.

Spring, summer, and autumn are the preferred seasons. Considering the frequent changes in both directions and grades, this might not be a particularly good snowshoe trail.

Mesa Trail South End

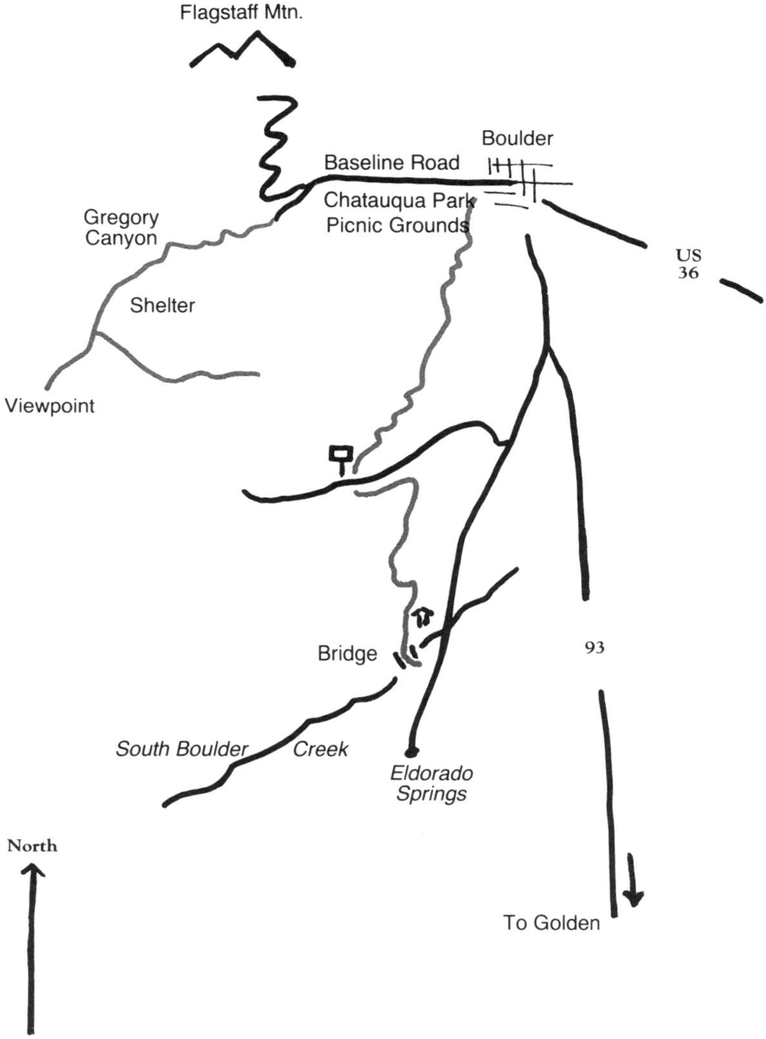

Flagstaff Mtn.

Boulder

Baseline Road

Gregory Canyon

Chatauqua Park Picnic Grounds

US 36

Shelter

Viewpoint

Bridge

93

South Boulder Creek

Eldorado Springs

North

To Golden

MESA TRAIL, SOUTH END

For those persons living along the front range metropolitan strip who would enjoy a hike in the late afternoon or early evening, a walk without a time-consuming drive into the mountains, the Mesa Trail is made to order.

Colorado State Highway 93 is the older way to go from Denver or Golden to Boulder. Just south of Boulder, across from the Marshall junction, County Highway 398 turns off to the southwest toward Eldorado Springs. Before you reach the village watch for the well-marked trailhead with parking below the road on the right or north side. Leave your car here.

Shoulder your pack and cross South Boulder Creek on the foot bridge. Go left at the junction just beyond the abandoned two-story stone house. Follow the path, narrow at this point, to the north as it climbs up through the meadow. At the point where the path intersects with a graded road, turn left on the road and walk past the Mesa Trail marker. Barely past the sign the foot path begins again. Turn right onto the path and continue up the series of switchbacks.

Here the trail becomes level as it traverses a pretty meadow. From here you get an attractive view of the north side of Denver as well as of the plains to the east. You have a choice when you come to the place where the trail intersects a second road. If you continue uphill to the left it will take you into Boulder, eventually. A turn to the right leads you back down to the trailhead on South Boulder Creek, but by a completely different route. Also at this junction, if time permits, cross the road and go up to the large rock outcroppings for an attractive picnic or snack stop. Return to your car by either of the two routes.

Near Boulder, the Mesa Trail wanders across the foothills.

Another section of Mesa Trail.

We think that spring or autumn are the most comfortable times for walking the Mesa Trail. Because of its relatively low altitude summer days can become a bit tepid here. In winter, snowshoeing is a possibility unless the foothills winds are blowing a gale across Boulder.

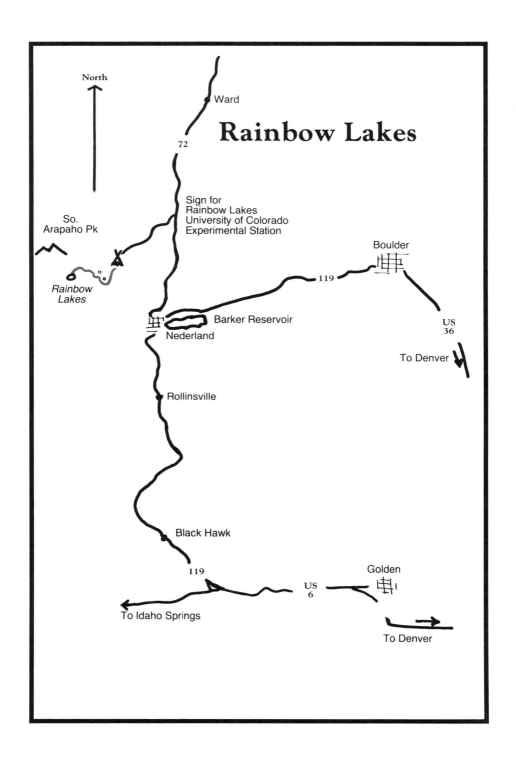

North

Ward

Rainbow Lakes

72

So.
Arapaho Pk

Sign for
Rainbow Lakes
University of Colorado
Experimental Station

Boulder

*Rainbow
Lakes*

119

Barker Reservoir

US
36

Nederland

To Denver

Rollinsville

Black Hawk

Golden

119

US
6

To Idaho Springs

To Denver

RAINBOW LAKES

Every book of this type should include at least one pretty hike that is really easy, a brief walk for the beginner who has not made up his or her mind about this hiking business. Short hikes are also useful as a first walk of the season or as a medium for breaking in a new pair of boots. Rainbow Lakes meets all of these qualifications.

US 36, the Denver–Boulder Turnpike, runs northwest from Denver to Boulder. Follow Colorado State Highway 119 from Boulder up Boulder Canyon to Nederland. Now turn north on State Highway 72 to the Rainbow Lakes–University of Colorado Experimental Station sign. A somewhat longer but more scenic approach may be taken by following West 6th Avenue out of Denver to Golden. Then take US 6 up Clear Creek Canyon to the forks where Colorado State Highway 119 begins. Follow 119 through Black Hawk and Nederland to the previously described sign.

Now follow the graded road west, keeping left at the University of Colorado facility sign. From this point to the 10,000 foot high Rainbow Lakes campground, the road is bumpy but not dangerous. No drinking water is available here so be sure to carry your own supply. There are only sixteen camping spaces here, so park in one of the designated parking areas for hikers.

From this point to the end of the trail is an easy mile. The path climbs moderately at first, then it runs up and down a series of gentle grades, passing two pretty little lakes, ending at a third. Where the trail traverses rocky areas be sure to watch carefully as the path really is not very distinct. It ends in a boulder pile that provides a nice view of the last lake.

If you want to do it, hike on up to timberline and the

snow fields. The distance is about one additional mile through sparse growths of evergreen trees. Keep the lake in sight to avoid needless wandering about when you are ready to return to the trail.

The dominant mountain that looms up behind the lake is 13,397 foot South Arapaho peak. Summer and autumn would be the preferred seasons for this easy walk.

The path up to Rainbow Lakes is both short and easy.

Here is the larger of the Rainbow Lakes.

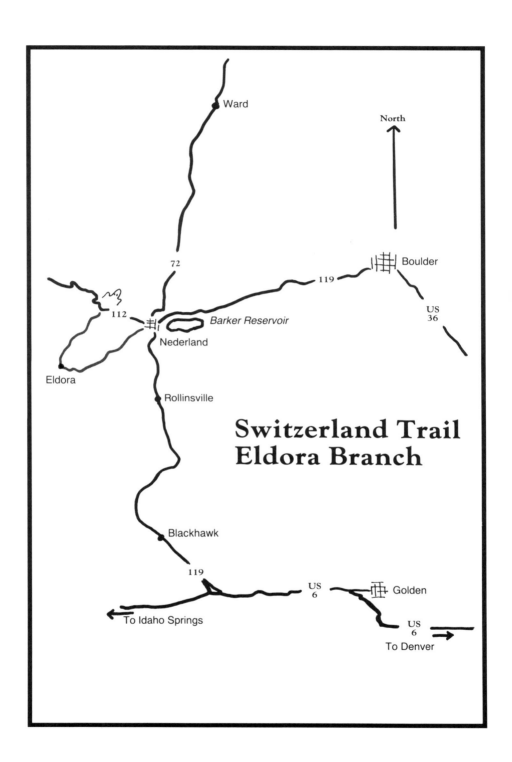

Ward

North

72

119 Boulder

US
36

112

Barker Reservoir

Eldora

Nederland

Rollinsville

Switzerland Trail
Eldora Branch

Blackhawk

119

US
6   Golden

To Idaho Springs

US
6
To Denver

SWITZERLAND TRAIL,
ELDORA BRANCH

Although nothing along this trail bears any resemblance to Swiss scenery, the country it traverses is, nevertheless, quite lovely. Its grade was once a railroad route. It was completed in 1881 and was called the Greeley, Salt Lake and Pacific. Until a flood damaged it in 1886 it carried freight, ores, and passengers to and from a number of mining communities in the western part of Boulder County.

After the flood had subsided the line was rebuilt as the Denver, Boulder and Western. Still later it was reorganized as the Colorado and Northwestern. But irrespective of the name changes, passengers always referred to it as the Switzerland Trail until it was abandoned in 1919. After the tracks were removed, much of its right of way became graded county roads that still wind about through Boulder County. Some of the other sections are currently on private land and are inaccessible, but the section described here is open to public use.

From Boulder, Colorado State Highway 119 will take you to Nederland. From Nederland drive west on Roosevelt National Forest Road 112 which will take you to the abandoned site of the town of Cardinal. The road is graded. It leaves the western edge of Nederland and goes generally uphill. In earlier times this grade was called the Coon Trail. Stop at Cardinal, the first group of buildings along the road.

Park here, put on your boots, and pack and walk south across the creek. Bushwhack uphill beyond the creek to the old railroad grade. Now begin walking generally southwest, left, along the trail. Although the route wanders somewhat, it goes mostly southwest until it turns west around the hills to enter the town of

Several hikers enjoy the Eldora Branch in autumn.

The Eldora Branch of the Switzerland Trail involves only a four
percent grade.

Eldora. There are a couple of places where railroad crews filled cuts and built trestles. These are obscure and you could miss them, so watch carefully. From Cardinal to Eldora the distance is just over two miles. At Eldora you have a choice between returning or making this a two car shuttle with one vehicle parked previously at Eldora.

Our chief reason for recommending this short trail is the profuse stands of brilliant yellow aspen trees that have grown up along both sides of the old grade, making this a really beautiful walk when the colors change in late September. Summer hikes are fine here, but autumn is really special.

Boulder
COUNTY

Since the ptarmigan is unable to fly, it assumes a rock-like camouflage in summer and a snow-white plumage in winter. The ptarmigan lives on Colorado's high peaks in the Arctic Alpine Zone.

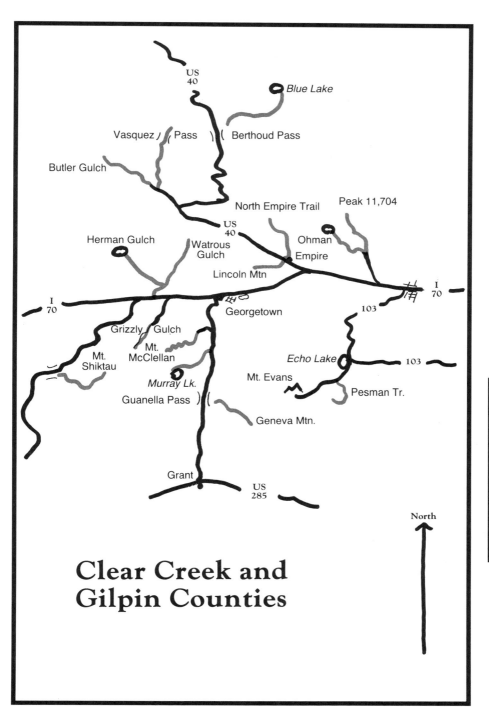

US
40

Blue Lake

Vasquez / (Pass) (Berthoud Pass

Butler Gulch

North Empire Trail

Peak 11,704

US
40

Herman Gulch

Watrous
Gulch

Ohman

Empire

Lincoln Mtn

I
70

I
70

Grizzly / Gulch

Georgetown

103

Mt.
McClellan

Mt.
Shiktau

Echo Lake

103

Murray Lk.

Mt. Evans

Pesman Tr.

Guanella Pass) (

Geneva Mtn.

Grant

US
285

North

Clear Creek and
Gilpin Counties

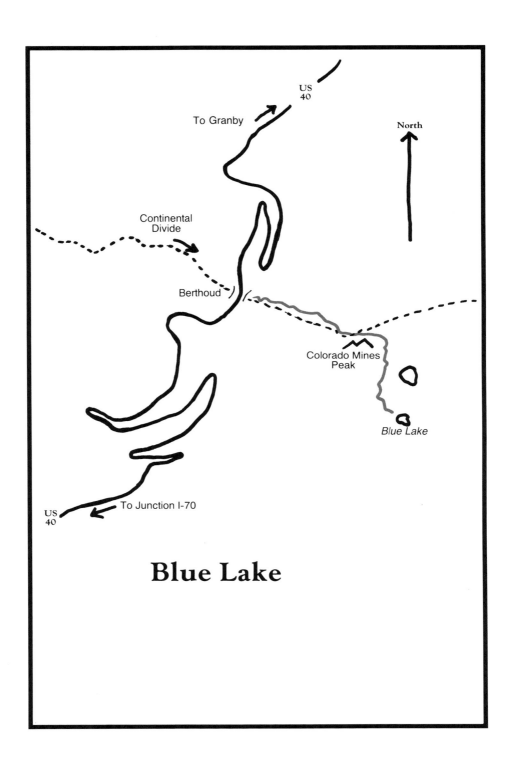

US
40

To Granby

North

Continental
Divide

Berthoud

Colorado Mines
Peak

Blue Lake

US
40
To Junction I-70

Blue Lake

BLUE LAKE

In common with several other states, Colorado has more than one Blue Lake. This one is located in the Berthoud Pass area, well above timberline. It is reached by driving west of Denver on Interstate 70 and US 40 to the 11,313 foot high top of Berthoud Pass. Leave your car at the south end of the parking area on the east side of the highway. An unimproved road begins at this point, providing access to the phone company relay that sends the signal from Denver to Squaw Mountain to Mines Peak and beyond, splitting to Vail and Granby.

Walk up this road as far as the third switchback, leave the grade and begin walking up across the tundra to the east. No trail exists on this ridge. Continue walking uphill toward the broad ridge to the right or east of Colorado Mines Peak. If you really watch carefully, you can pick up the trail here. It is a dim one, showing little evidence of use. If you cannot locate it, head toward the rock pile on the next ridge to the west. Here the path is somewhat more visible.

Turn toward the left at the rock pile and contour around Colorado Mines Peak, making your way down toward the two lakes in the valley below. One of the accompanying photographs was made from this location. Beyond the growth of low evergreens is Blue Lake, fed by the melting snow that lies above it. From here down to the lake the trail is quite evident but rather narrow. Blue Lake is the smaller and more distant of the two lakes.

We feel that it works best to return to the pile of rocks on the ridge for your lunch stop. Hiking up a steep grade following even a modest repast can be an uncomfortable experience. As you leave the aforementioned outcropping, look ahead to the west, get the path in view and head for it.

87

In this above-timberline view, the dim trail to Blue Lake is seen wandering across the tundra.

Looking down into the cirque, the arrow points to Blue Lake's location.

In July and August the columbine, yellow and red Indian paintbrush, bistort, and purple pincushion are abundant and very colorful on this crest. Looking off toward the south, the American Metals Climax complex fills the valley below Jones and Vasquez Passes. Continue on toward the west but do not go downhill. As you reach the crest of the ridge, the summit of Berthoud Pass and US 40 come into view below you.

Now head generally toward the top of the hill, picking up the telephone maintenance road for the return to your car. The total walking distance has been five miles. July, August, and September are our preferred months for this above timberline hike. Because nearly all of this terrain is well above the tree line, you should watch the clouds. Avoid at all costs any hint of an electrical storm. Inclement weather can move in quickly at this altitude.

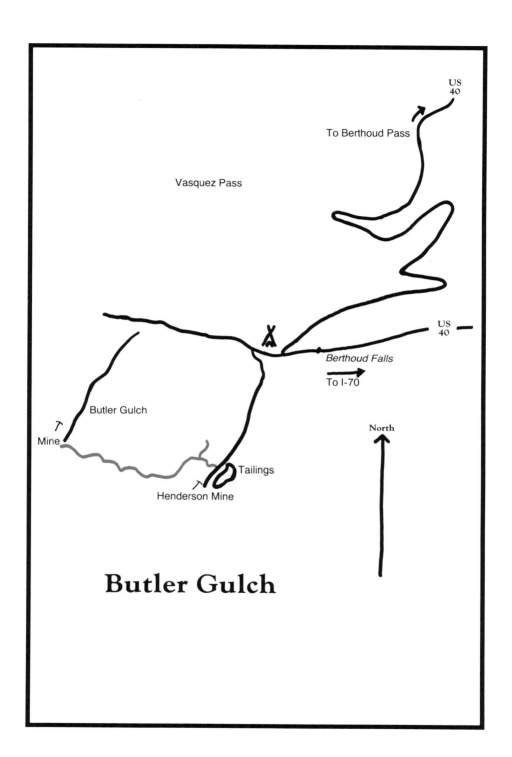

US
40

To Berthoud Pass

Vasquez Pass

US
40

Berthoud Falls

To I-70

North

Butler Gulch

Mine

Tailings

Henderson Mine

Butler Gulch

BUTLER GULCH

Butler Gulch is not one of the more widely known hiking paths in the Denver area, but it is a very pretty place and the trail is neither difficult nor particularly long. In season it offers pretty wild flowers, a nice little stream and both evergreen and deciduous trees. All of Butler Gulch lies within the Arapaho National Forest.

Depending on traffic and your own driving habits, just over an hour is required to reach the trailhead from Denver. Take Interstate 70 west past Idaho Springs to the Empire and Berthoud Pass exit. Leave the freeway at this point. You are now on US 40. Barely past Berthoud Falls the highway makes an abrupt hairpin turn to the right. Here another road goes straight ahead toward Jones Pass and the Henderson Mine of the American Metals Climax Company. Take this latter road, but do not drive up toward Jones Pass. Instead, park on the graded road across from the Henderson Mine. You will find enough space on the left side for several cars.

Begin walking up the hill and go left or west at the fork. Quite often there has been a Forest Service barricade here to keep motorized vehicles out. You are now on an old mining and logging road that was used in the last century. Rather abruptly the trail turns south. In soggy places it has been corduroyed with logs laid at right angles across the path. Twice you will cross streams on improvised bridges of fallen trees. The dense growth of evergreen trees makes this a comfortably shady trail. Below the path a rather noisy but very pretty little stream parallels your route at this point.

Soon the tree growth becomes sparse and you enter Colorado's Arctic–Alpine Zone. Here at timberline in July we have found many colorful and delicate wild flowers including the columbine, bistort, and both the white and blue penstemon. Once you are above the tree line, at the point where the trail turns west again, look behind you at Colorado Mines Peak adjacent to Berthoud Pass. To its left in the lower saddle is Vasquez Pass, the subject of a later hike in this section.

There are a couple of additional stream crossings up here on the tundra. If the weather permits, you could go on beyond the end of the trail in the high basin. But if clouds begin to gather you would be wise not to continue beyond this point. The trail ends at about the 12,000 foot level in a cirque where an old mine perches above its yellowed tailings dump. To its left you will see an extensive snow field that is perfect for glissading on a plastic sheet. Beware of rocks beneath the snow. On the top of the dump there sits a quite old and badly rusted car of undetermined origin. We speculate that whoever drove it up here was a victim of mental clumsiness. Apart from this, we enjoy using this pretty basin as our lunch stop.

At this point you have now hiked approximately two and a half miles, and you should return by the same route. Snowshoeing might be possible on the protected sections of this trail but we have never tried it. We feel that the time span from late June through autumn is the preferred one for a rewarding walk in Butler Gulch.

This picture looks back toward the trailhead. The Butler Gulch path shows at the lower right.

Snow fields abound on the Butler Gulch trail during most of the hiking season.

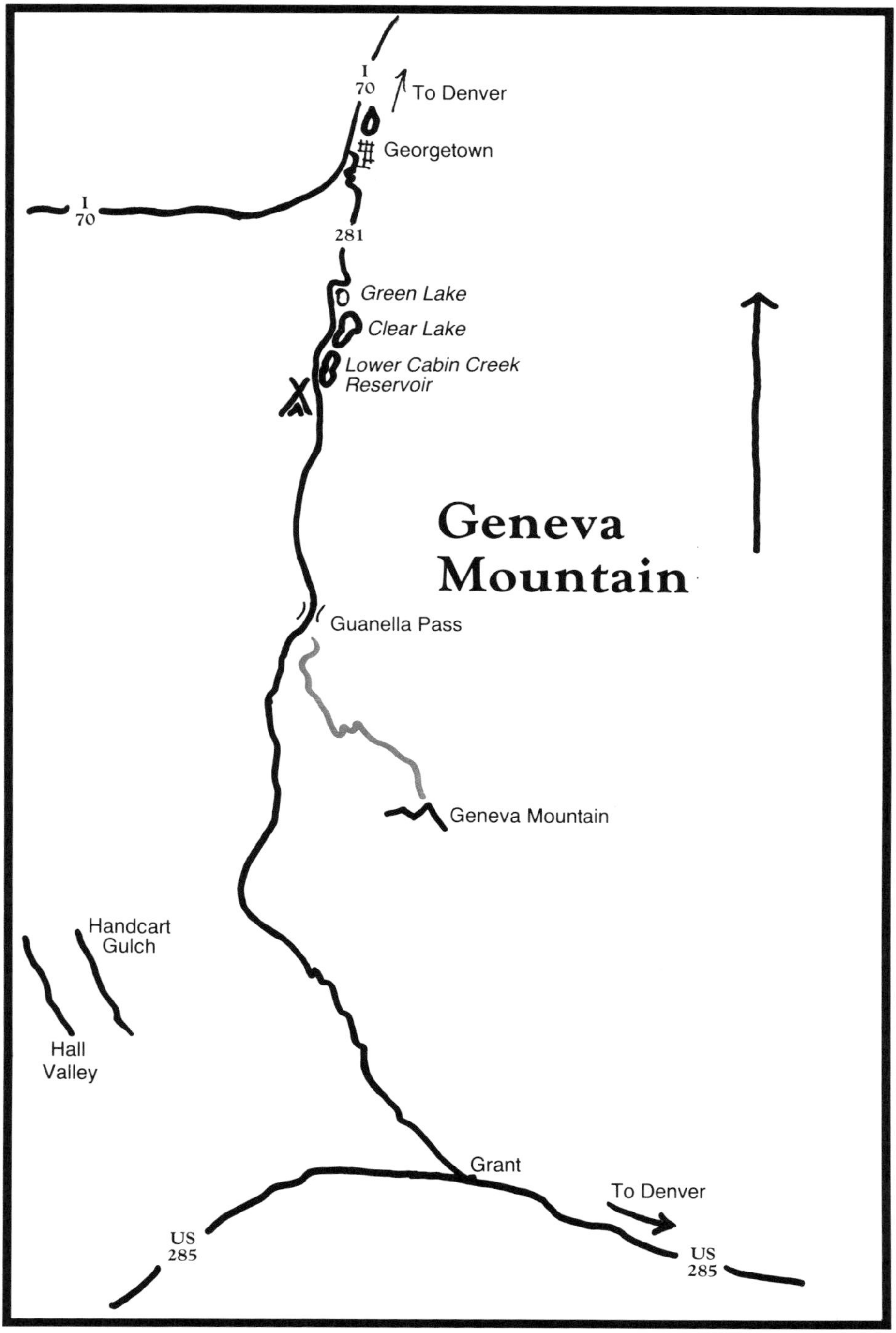
I 70
To Denver
Georgetown
I 70
281
Green Lake
Clear Lake
Lower Cabin Creek Reservoir
Geneva Mountain
Guanella Pass
Geneva Mountain
Handcart Gulch
Hall Valley
Grant
To Denver
US 285
US 285

GENEVA MOUNTAIN

Here is another of those hikes that is completely above timberline. The Geneva Mountain Trail lies entirely within the Pike National Forest. Start from the town of Grant on US 285 and turn north on the road that parallels Geneva Creek. Drive to the top of 11,665 foot Guanella Pass. An equally satisfactory approach begins at Georgetown and follows South Clear Creek up beyond the Public Service Cabin Creek facility to the top of Guanella Pass. Park in the space on the east side where the road crosses the summit. A trail, double rutted in places, leads off across the tundra toward the south.

Before you are out of sight of the parking area, the trail forks. We usually follow the right branch which climbs up over the ridge. The left fork circles around the hill, is a bit longer but joins up with the original trail once more on the other side. If you look off to the south from the top of the first hill, three peaks of about equal height are visible. Geneva Mountain is the farthest to the left of the three.

From this point you need only to follow the trail. Since this path wanders around considerably, several short cuts to the left are possible and will save many steps. However, always keep the main trail in sight and be sure to return to it after each digression. You can skirt that first summit of the three in this way, picking up the trail again in the next saddle.

The second summit is called Hill 12,179. From its rocky top you can see Square Top Peak, backed by the Guanella summit. To its left the red hued valleys are Handcart Gulch and Hall Valley, while the large open area still further to the left is South Park. Almost directly to the east is 14,060 foot Mount Bierstadt. Behind it, the larger mountain that peeks out along its

95

From the dim path along the ridge, Geneva Mountain can be seen in the center of the picture.

A rewarding mountain view can be enjoyed from the above timberline summit of Geneva Mountain.

right side is Mount Evans. South of it are the double summits of Mount Epaulet. The rounded peak to the south of Epaulet is Mount Rosalie. If it happens to be a windy day, the rocks here on the summit provide a somewhat sheltered lunch stop.

From this point the route to Geneva Mountain is fully visible. Walk down through the grassy saddle and up to your destination. Pike National Forest maps show this trail continuing on down the ridge with a fork to the southwest that takes you down Scott Gomer Creek to the Burning Bear Campground. A second fork crosses to the southeast over Tahana Mountain and goes down to the end of the Deer Creek Valley road. Both of these digressions would be candidates for two car hikes.

From Guanella Pass to Geneva Mountain and the return involves a walk of six miles with an elevation gain of less than 1,000 feet. Late summer and autumn would be the most acceptable seasons for walking this exposed ridge. But if the weather sours, turn back at once.

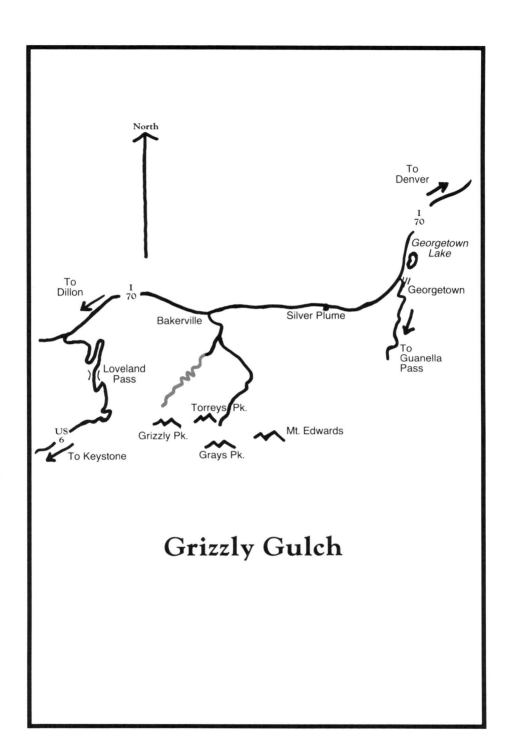

North

To
Denver

I
70

Georgetown
Lake

To
Dillon

I
70

Georgetown

Bakerville

Silver Plume

To
Guanella
Pass

Loveland
Pass

Torreys Pk.

US
6

Grizzly Pk.

Mt. Edwards

Grays Pk.

To Keystone

Grizzly Gulch

GRIZZLY GULCH

To find Grizzly Gulch, drive west from Denver on Interstate 70 past Georgetown and Silver Plume to the Bakerville exit. Cross the freeway by way of the overpass to the south side. Behind the remains of the old lodge a graveled road turns back toward the east, then runs south as it winds steeply up the gulch. When you have driven about two miles, watch for a road cutting off to the right. It drops quickly down toward Quayle Creek. Park on the right side of the road and hike across the bridge. This trail can be driven in a 4-wheel drive car for some distance, so be prepared to share the right of way.

Several crossings of Quayle Creek are necessary and you will probably encounter some mud here and there. In places the path becomes quite steep as you climb upward through a dense growth of evergreen trees. There is at least one side trail, but it returns to the main path in about a half mile. Higher up the trees become more sparse as both Grizzly and 14,264 foot Torreys Peaks come into view. Here is a good vantage point for any number of attractive photographic possibilities. Wild flowers are abundant in season.

The first known attempt to tunnel beneath the Continental Divide originated in Grizzly Gulch. If it had been carried through to completion the western portal would have emerged in the upper reaches of Peru Creek, not far from Argentine Pass. When finished it would have been 25,200 feet long. Some exploratory work was done at both ends, but the critical center portion was never cut through. By 1892 the workers were in 400 feet on the east side and 1,400 feet on the west approach. The spark plug for this ambitious project was a dreamer named Mark M. "Brick" Pomeroy, who earned his nickname by building a home in Denver from that material. Pomeroy called his dream enterprise the Atlantic–Pacific Tunnel. It would have saved 100 miles of the distance from Denver to Leadville.

When they were first offered to the public, shares of stock in the Atlantic–Pacific Tunnel sold for $2.50 each. Finally the tunnel became just another mining property. In fact, it had cut through some 200 known mineral fissures. Available information is conflicting about which of the various mine holes in the gulch had been the Pomeroy property, so beware of "authorities." The excellent USGS maps do not attempt to identify it.

If you hike all the way to the 11,300 foot high head of the gulch the elevation gain will be about 1,000 feet in two and a half miles, making a round trip distance of five miles. Summer and autumn are our preferred seasons for this walk. Visible snowslide paths should rule out snowshoeing, particularly in the upper reaches of the gulch.

In the appendix of his fine book *The Great Gates*, author Marshall Sprague describes an often surveyed but never completed crossing of the Continental Divide called Grizzly Pass. Supposedly it would go up from near the end of the present hiking pass to cross the range through the saddle beside Grizzly Peak. Allegedly there is a path of sorts up there somewhere.

Ascending Grizzle Gulch, the narrow hiking path is visible in the lower right foreground.

At this point the Grizzle Gulch Trail follows a pretty stream.

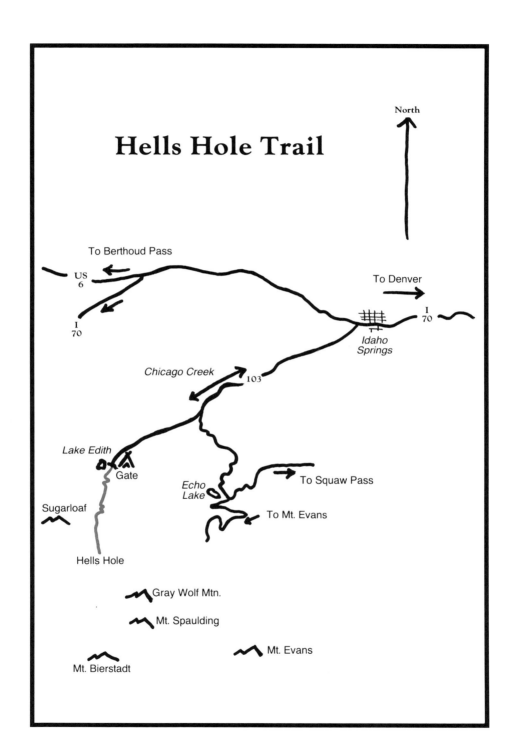

Hells Hole Trail

North

To Berthoud Pass

US 6

To Denver

I 70

I 70

Idaho Springs

Chicago Creek

103

Lake Edith

Gate

Echo Lake

To Squaw Pass

Sugarloaf

To Mt. Evans

Hells Hole

Gray Wolf Mtn.

Mt. Spaulding

Mt. Evans

Mt. Bierstadt

HELLS HOLE TRAIL

Surely a more appropriate name could have been found for this pristine high mountain valley. Hells Hole is a near timberline bowl nestled under the southern slopes of Mount Evans and Mount Bierstadt. Curiously, the trail stops some distance short of the location designated on USGS maps as Hells Hole.

To experience the pleasure of this rewarding hike, you drive south of Idaho Springs on State Highway 103, the West Chicago Creek–Echo Lake road. At the point where the highway doubles back abruptly to the left, leave the pavement and continue straight ahead on the graded road to the West Chicago Creek campground. Park in the designated area between the campground and the picnic area. Walk past the Forest Service gate and through the picnic facilities to the trailhead at the south edge of the circle. Although not designated by name at this writing, this is the beginning of the trail to Hells Hole.

Short steep grades are interspersed among relatively level stretches as the path gains about 1,300 feet of elevation in four miles. You will cross small streams that are tributary to West Chicago Creek at several points. There is a single log and dirt bridge while the other crossings are made by stepping on well-placed large rocks.

The first half of the trail traverses a striking area of stately aspen trees. Wild flowers, including the columbine, are abundant in season. At the higher elevations the deciduous trees are left behind as the path continues upward into a growth of evergreens. Looking back toward the north the Continental Divide, dominated by James Peak, comes into view. Several trail breaks have been placed along the way to discourage the prohibited motorized vehicles.

A heavenly panorama may be seen from the Hells Hole Trail.

The easy trail to Hells Hole traverses the center of this picture.

As you top the ridge, 14,262 foot high Mount Evans and 14,060 foot Mount Bierstadt loom up ahead of you. The pyramid-shaped peak to the right or west is called Sugarloaf. Many lofty but dead trees offer unusual photographic compositions to the camera enthusiast. At an altitude of some 11,200 feet the trail ends on a pretty ridge. Here the area is dominated by a modest growth of big evergreens, creating a cool and scenic lunch stop.

If you maintain a steady and sensible pace, it requires about two hours to reach this point. The total distance, round trip, is about eight miles. Because of the altitude you should consider this as a midsummer or autumn trail. Also, plan on hitting the trail early in order to reach your lunch stop by the noon hour since afternoon showers are common at this elevation during both of the recommended seasons.

Herman Gulch

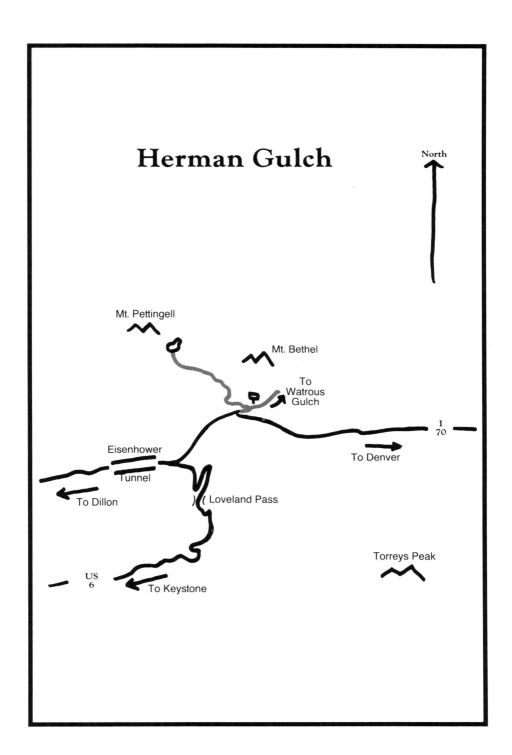

North

Mt. Pettingell

Mt. Bethel

To Watrous Gulch

I 70

To Denver

Eisenhower Tunnel

To Dillon

Loveland Pass

Torreys Peak

US 6

To Keystone

HERMAN GULCH

Watrous and Herman Gulches share the same trail-head. To get there follow the directions given in the Watrous Gulch chapter. Briefly, drive west beyond Silver Plume on Interstate 70 and on past the Bakerville exit. Leave the highway at the next exit, currently unmarked, and park on the north side of the road by the ridge of gravel. Cross the ridge and walk back toward the east on a partly overgrown road for about an eighth of a mile. Turn left and begin hiking uphill at the "Watrous Gulch–Herman Gulch" sign. Go about an eighth of a mile up this path to the point where it intersects an old double rut trail. Now turn abruptly left and begin walking uphill toward the west.

For the first half mile or so the old road intersects a grove of evergreens as it follows the contours of a moderately steep grade. Gradually the path narrows. By the time it emerges into a meadow it has become a simple path. It wanders in and out of groves of trees, crosses little streams and gains its altitude gradually. Here and there you will notice side paths leaving the main trail. Most of these are of fairly recent vintage and represent random efforts of hikers to avoid marshy spots. Virtually all of them eventually wander back to the principal path.

When you have walked about a mile, rugged vistas of the Continental Divide begin to open up. Torreys Peak and some of its lesser neighbors now loom up behind you. The dominant mountain on the left is Mt. Bethel. The largest of the snowy peaks at the head of the valley is Mt. Pettingell. Below it, and slightly to the east is Lake Herman which lies at the head of the gulch.

The total round trip walking distance to and from the lake is just over six very pleasant miles. Summer and

At timberline, hikers walk along a section of the Herman Gulch path.
The view looks toward the east.

In the upper reaches of Herman Gulch, the path traverses
a boulder field.

autumn are the preferred seasons for this walk. In winter Herman Gulch becomes a fine trail for snowshoeing. For many years the Colorado Mountain Club has used it for their beginning trips. In summer some species of mushrooms grow in the gulch. Likewise, the gulch is a good place for amateur botanists who enjoy our colorful wild flowers.

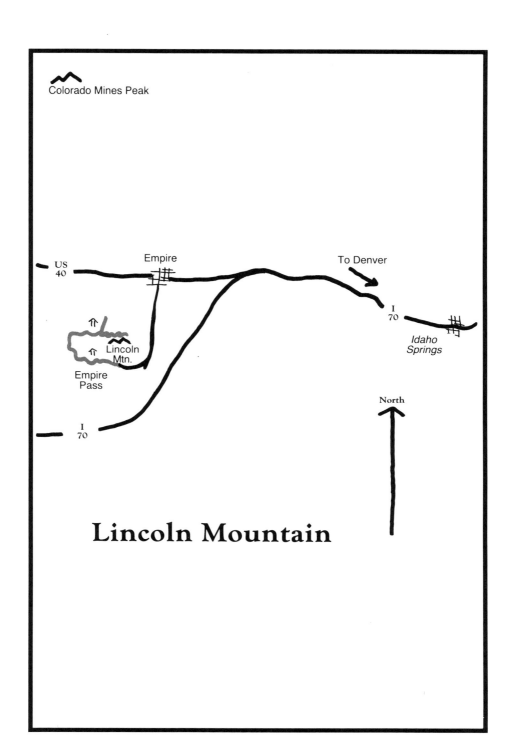

Colorado Mines Peak

US
40

Empire

To Denver

I
70

Idaho
Springs

Lincoln
Mtn.

Empire
Pass

I
70

North

Lincoln Mountain

LINCOLN MOUNTAIN

Landmarks are often given common names such as Clear Creek, Mount Baldy, or Blue Lake. Following this custom, Colorado has several mountains that were named for our sixteenth president. Best known of the group is 14,286 foot Mount Lincoln near Alma. Lincoln Mountain rises to a less pretentious 10,146 feet above sea level. It is located in Clear Creek County, near the town of Empire.

To take this hike follow Interstate 70 west from Denver to the Empire–Berthoud Pass exit, which is US 40. Halfway through Empire turn left or south and follow the dirt road to the summit of old Union or Empire Pass. Do not start down the pass toward Georgetown. Instead, take the trail or road that bends to the right. Follow this road to the fork beside a cabin and park in the cleared area.

Begin walking up the left fork and cross Bard Creek. The trail is steep and has some switchbacks. At the next fork, beside a cabin with a large chimney, turn uphill to the right. You will pass the dumps of the Robinson and Lincoln Mines, both inactive now. Just beyond the second dump the path forks once more. Turn right here onto Lincoln Mountain. When you have reached the long tree lined ridge you are at the top. If you look down through the cleared area, the town of Empire is visible in the valley below.

Looking off to the north you can see Berthoud Pass and Colorado Mines Peak with its relay to the summit. Your return is by way of the same route in reverse. Total walking distance for this walk is about six miles with 1,200 feet of elevation gain. Because deep snows remain among dense tree growths in spring, the best seasons for hiking up Lincoln Mountain would be summer and autumn.

In the late spring, this is one of the views from the
Lincoln Mountain Trail.

From the top of Lincoln Mountain we look down on Interstate 70
and the village of Empire.

The Continental Divide looms up in the distance as seen from the top of Lincoln Mountain.

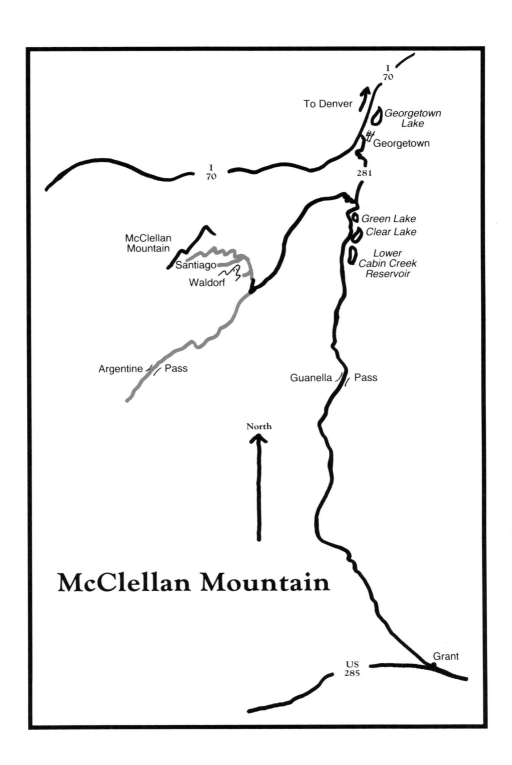

McClellan Mountain

To Denver

I 70

Georgetown Lake

Georgetown

281

Green Lake
Clear Lake

Lower
Cabin Creek
Reservoir

McClellan
Mountain

Santiago

Waldorf

Argentine Pass

Guanella Pass

North

US 285

Grant

McCLELLAN MOUNTAIN

The McClellan Mountain Trail is actually the abandoned grade of the Argentine Central Railroad. By ascending to the summit of McClellan Mountain, the narrow gauge Argentine Central gained the distinction of being the highest operating railroad in the United States. The McClellan Ridge rises to an elevation of 13,644 feet. It is just north of the Continental Divide.

Edward Wilcox, a retired Methodist clergyman, had mined and prospered at nearby Waldorf. From his profits Wilcox financed construction of the line during 1905–06. It still carried passengers as far as its lofty end of tracks until it was abandoned in 1919. In deference to Wilcox's former profession, this was the only railroad in America that never operated on Sundays.

To begin this hike, drive to Georgetown and take the switchback road up from the south end of the town. This is Clear Creek Highway 281. Follow this road south past Green Lake and toward Guanella Pass. Now watch for a junction where a road branches abruptly to the right or west. A sign marked "Waldorf" identifies this road.

Although this is not a great road, it is passable for most cars as far as the abandoned town of Waldorf. There the road splits. The narrow trail straight ahead climbs steeply up to Argentine Pass. The other trail swings back to the right and heads up toward the McClellan Ridge. Park here and begin walking.

Less than a mile above Waldorf the road splits again. Continue straight ahead at this junction. A left turn here will put you in what remains of the ghost town of Santiago. If time and the weather permit, you might enjoy the short three-quarter-mile detour into Santiago to see the cabins and the huge old Santiago Mill.

Otherwise continue up the long series of four lengthy switchbacks to the McClellan summit. You will likely experience a shortness of breath as the altitude is high here. So stop and get a breath frequently; it makes the walk more enjoyable.

Virtually all of this hike is on above timberline tundra. Waldorf's altitude is 11,666 feet above sea level. Residents of the town used to boast about having the highest post office in the States. So be prepared. Carry rain gear and a hat. Better yet, don't go up if the sky looks threatening. The long, ridged summit of McClellan is no place to get stranded in an electrical storm.

On a clear day the view from the ridge is one of Colorado's finest. From the top you can look out from the edge of sheer cliffs that form the eastern wall of Stevens Gulch. Far below the road along the spine of the gulch comes up from Bakerville. Those two big peaks are Grays and Torreys, both over 14,000 feet high. To their right is 13,070 foot Mount Kelso. On a clear day the foot trail leading up from the head of Stevens Gulch to the summit of Grays Peak is clearly visible.

From Waldorf the distance up to the top of Mount McClellan is just over six miles, with some 2000 feet of elevation gain. Since 4-wheel drive vehicles use this trail, you may find that you are not alone, particularly on week-ends. The only seasons that are satisfactory for this very scenic hike are late summer and early autumn. Be sure to carry a camera.

The Argentine Central Railroad once traversed this trail on
Mt. McClellan.

From the summit of Mt. McClellan, the view is magnificant
in all directions.

117

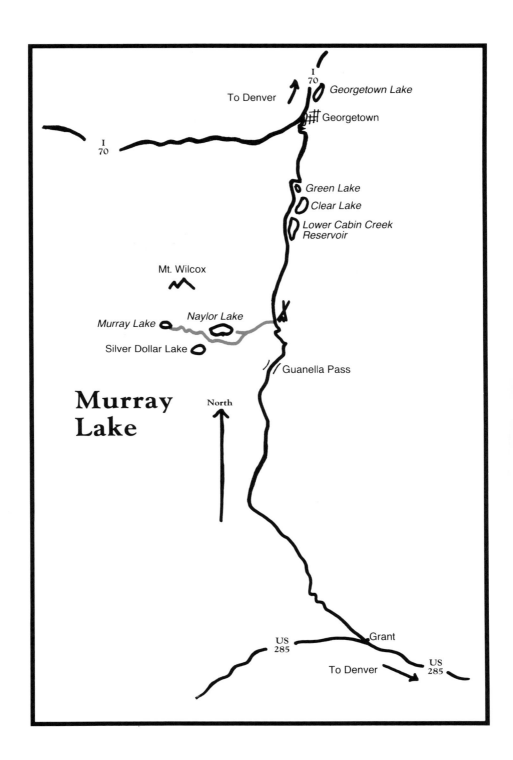

Murray Lake

MURRAY LAKE

Murray Lake is located within the Arapaho National Forest in an above timberline basin at an elevation of 12,400 feet. It is near the western edge of Clear Creek County and just below the Continental Divide. Argentine Peak, 13,738 feet high, looms above the lake to the northwest and 13,408 foot high Mount Wilcox is directly to the north.

The route to Murray Lake uses the Silver Dollar Lake trailhead. From the Denver area, drive west on Interstate 70 and exit at Georgetown. Follow Rose Street through the town. A series of abrupt switchbacks will take you past the Georgetown Reservoir and Green Lake and on toward Guanella Pass. Continue on past the Clear Lake Campground. Just beyond the Guanella Pass Campground watch for an abrupt curve where a steep road heads uphill to your right. This half mile long spur is rocky in places but passable. It ends at the Silver Dollar Lake trailhead where there is parking space for several cars.

Follow the well-defined path as it climbs up through a series of thin evergreen stands toward timberline. The lake below the trail on your right is called Naylor Lake. Because this path begins above 10,000 feet and climbs past 11,950 foot high Silver Dollar Lake, winter snows can remain well into July. Here and there it may be necessary to cross a snow field. We have almost always seen an abundant growth of colorful wild flowers along this trail. At Silver Dollar Lake, follow the path around to the north along the right shore. Finally, walk up the tundra slope to the northwest to Murray Lake.

From late July through mid-September is usually the best time for this walk, depending on the ever-present possibility of an early snow. From the trailhead and

The trail to Murray Lake is a particularly scenic one.

Murray Lake lies nestled in this high altitude cirque.

return, the round trip distance is just over three miles. Since you will be above the tree line for most of the way to and from the lake, be wary of summer electrical storms.

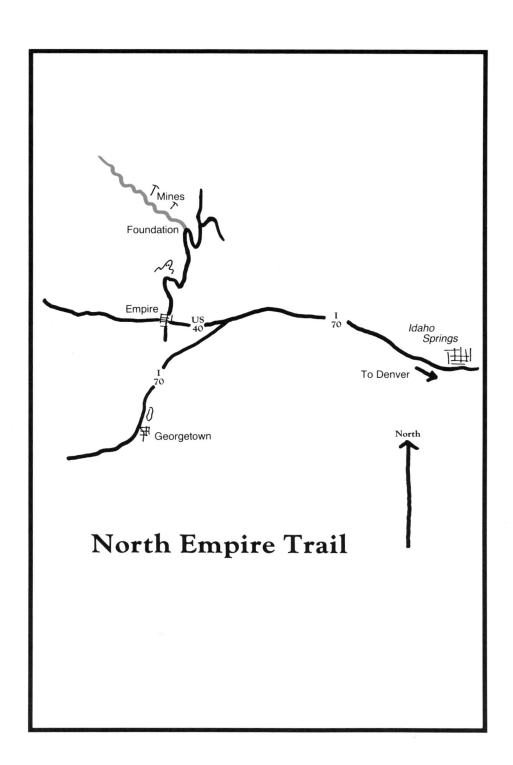

North Empire Trail

NORTH EMPIRE TRAIL

The North Empire trail lies within the Arapaho National Forest. To reach the trailhead, drive west from the Denver area on Interstate 70. Leave the freeway at US 40, the Empire exit. When you reach the town of Empire, turn uphill to your right in the center of town onto the graded road that follows North Empire Creek. When you have driven approximately a mile you will enter what remains of the ghost town of North Empire. This particular section of the road that you have followed from Empire up to North Empire was formerly described as "the longest main street in the country." In winter, coasting parties rode sleds and toboggans down the steep grade to Empire, a soul-shaking experience if one may believe old letters written by those persons who did it and survived.

Another mile will take you to a large foundation, visible on the left. Until recent years a large white two story boarding house stood here. It was built in the early 1870s to house miners who labored in the rich Conqueror Mine. A fire of undetermined origin destroyed the structure several years ago. Where the road makes a sharp switchback to the right, a path leads uphill toward the northwest. It ends at the Conqueror Mine property. Depending on the vehicle you are driving and the condition of the road beyond this curve. perhaps you should park here and begin walking.

The old road now runs south to about 9,500 feet of elevation, then turns north for some distance. Finally it turns toward the northwest, ending at about 10,500 feet above sea level. In general, the grades are gradual. As you can see by the ruts this was a wagon road at one time.

From the Conqueror to the point where the trail stops

This view looks back down toward the Clear Creek valley from a
point on the North Empire trail.

This portion of the North Empire Trail was a mining road
at one time.

the distance is just over two miles. From late June to early October this is a pleasant walk. At times you may find it necessary to share the right-of-way with 4-wheel drive cars. The return walk follows the same route.

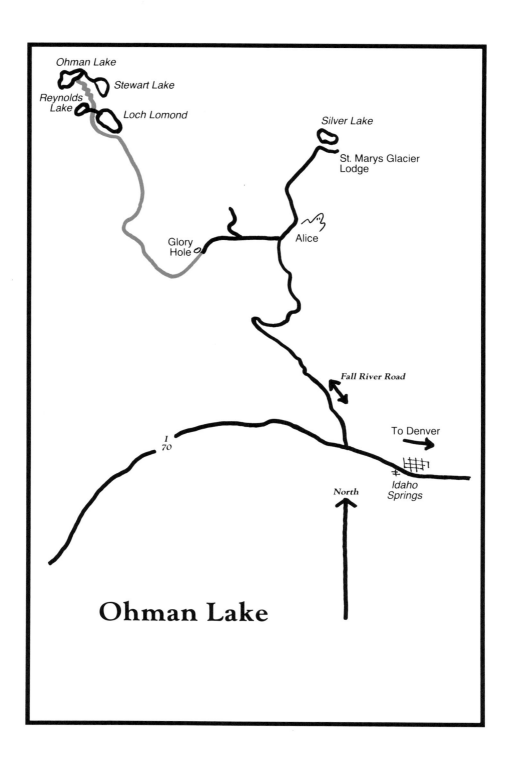

Ohman Lake

Ohman Lake

Stewart Lake

Reynolds Lake

Loch Lomond

Silver Lake

St. Marys Glacier Lodge

Glory Hole

Alice

Fall River Road

I 70

To Denver

North

Idaho Springs

OHMAN LAKE

Ohman Lake is just one of the multiplicity of pretty little high altitude lakes that are nestled among the lofty peaks of the Arapaho National Forest. It is close to the larger metropolitan areas and is very accessible for a short outing when time is precious.

To reach the trailhead take Interstate 70 to the Fall River exit, located just a mile west of Idaho Springs. Drive north up the partially paved Fall River road to the old ghost town of Alice. Turn left and go up hill past the little white school and continue on to the large cavity known as the Alice Glory Hole. Park in the turnout on the left side of the road just beyond the hole. Now walk along this road for a short distance to the first inter-section. Turn right at this fork and follow the narrow and sometimes steep 4-wheel drive trail up through a stand of evergreen trees.

Where the view opens up, the snow-capped peaks on the western horizon are Mount Eva, Mount Bancroft, Parrys and James Peaks. In the other direction Squaw and Chief Mountains and Mount Evans can be seen. At 11,200 feet of elevation you will come to a pretty lake called Loch Lomond. Here the 4-wheel drive road ends. Even in July there are snow banks around the shore, so walk to the left of the water. Just slightly uphill is the path you want. It takes you through dense willows, over a huge old rusty iron water conduit, and across icy little tributary streams.

Then abruptly the trail starts climbing very steeply up the hillside onto a tundra shelf that contains Reynolds and Stewart Lakes. The trail passes between these lakes, then climbs up over a bank of snow and traverses a small ridge to Ohman Lake.

We have found ice in this lake in both late July and in

early August. Drifts of snow remain until late in the season. So think of this as a late summer or early autumn outing. Because of the confining nature of the terrain a wide angle lens will yield better pictures. A 28mm lens works well for pictures at the lake. Due to the altitude, a warm jacket should be included in your pack. Round trip hiking distance is seven miles.

The Ohman Lake Trail passes a snow bridge.

Ohman Lake nestled in a deep glacial cirque.

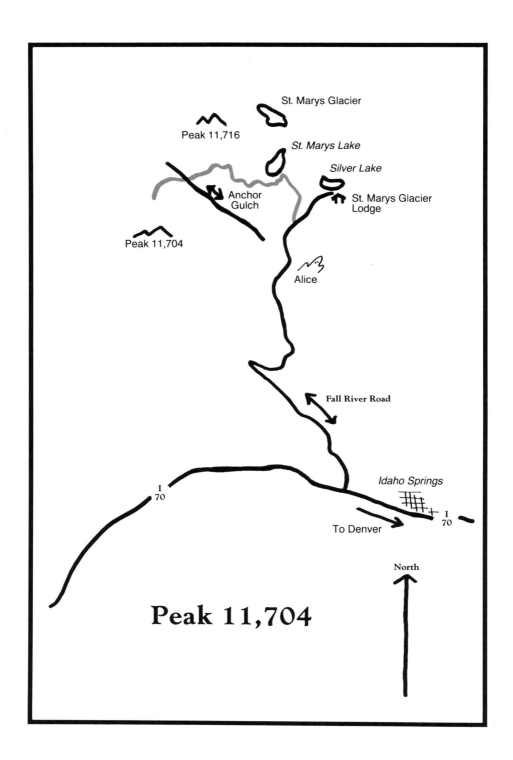

St. Marys Glacier

Peak 11,716

St. Marys Lake

Silver Lake

Anchor
Gulch

St. Marys Glacier
Lodge

Peak 11,704

Alice

Fall River Road

I
70

Idaho Springs

To Denver

I
70

North

Peak 11,704

PEAK 11,704

In any area that is as intensely mountainous as Colorado, there are many fine peaks that have never been named. The subject of this section is one such summit. All of Colorado's 14,000 foot peaks have names. Most, but not all, of the "thirteeners" have been identified, but many of the lower ones possess no formal designations other than their altitudes. Peak 11,704 deserves a name because its top can be reached with minimal effort and because the surrounding panorama is an outstanding one.

From the Denver area, drive west on Interstate 70 to the Fall River exit, just a mile west of Idaho Springs. Take the Fall River road, now partly paved, past the ghost town of Alice to the marked trailhead for St. Marys Lake and glacier. Park here and walk up to the lake. Instead of continuing toward the glacier, go to your left around the lake for a fifth of a mile to the large boulders. An arrow on the accompanying photograph shows the point at which you should leave the path and begin climbing.

There is no trail here, so just head steeply uphill toward the ridge. When you have reached what appeared to be the top you will see another ridge ahead of you that contains a dense growth of twisted bristlecone pine trees near its top. Now angle slightly to your right or north toward another of those unnamed mountains of 11,715 foot altitude. Keep to the left of this summit and you will find a faint path.

The path angles to the left across Anchor Gulch. Depending on the season, you may need to cross a large but firm snow field. Beyond the snow to the west there is a hill with a trail cut across its side. Walk toward this path and follow it to the top. A rock cairn marks the top

The arrow above St. Mary Lake indicates the starting point for the hike to Peak 11,704.

From the top of Peak 11,704, we look across at James Peak, above Loch Lomond.

of peak 11,704. Stop here for lunch, get your bearings for the return trip, and then enjoy the view. As you face the snow-crested peaks from your right or north they are James Peak, Mount Bancroft, Parrys Peak, Mount Eva, and Mount Flora off to the southwest. Loch Lomond is the large lake below James Peak. If you turn and look toward the south the town in the distant valley is Georgetown. Above it on the horizon are Grays and Torreys Peaks.

Due to the altitude and the potential for inclement weather, mid-summer and early autumn would be the best as well as the safest seasons for this hike. The return trip is by the same route that you followed to get up here, so take careful note of the more prominent landmarks, a good practice for any outing where there is not an established trail to follow. Be sure to carry binoculars and a camera with plenty of film when you visit Peak 11,704.

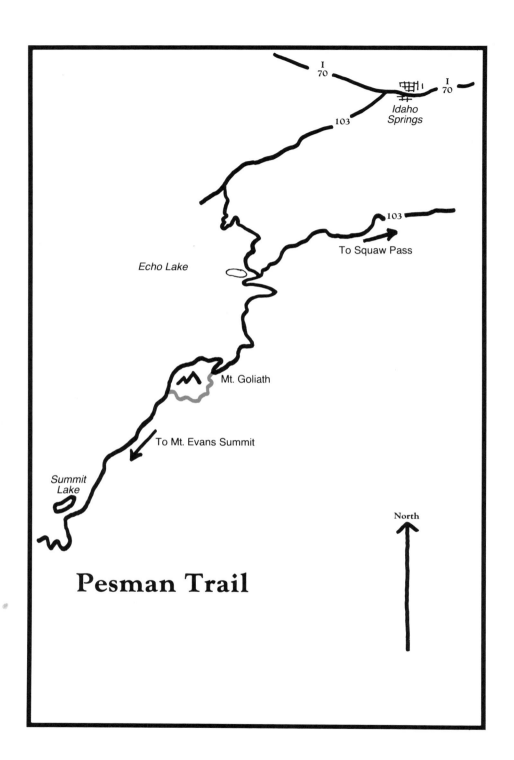

I 70

103

I 70

Idaho
Springs

103

To Squaw Pass

Echo Lake

Mt. Goliath

To Mt. Evans Summit

Summit
Lake

Pesman Trail

North

PESMAN TRAIL

By profession, M. Walter Pesman was a landscape architect who landscaped the grounds of several of Denver's schools. He was also an avid botanist, first chairman of the editorial committee of *The Green Thumb* magazine and author of *Meet The Natives*, one of the finest books ever written on identification of Colorado's wild flowers. Pesman was an active member and supporter of Denver's fine Botanic Gardens. Established in 1958, the Pesman Trail recognizes this man's many contributions to the botanical sciences.

This is neither a long nor a difficult trail, but all of it is located at or above the treeline, encompassing 160 acres at an altitude that ranges between 11,500 and 12,150 feet of elevation. The Pesman Trail is a self-guiding nature trail that specializes in plants typical of the Arctic–Alpine Zone. Located on the slope of Mount Goliath, west of Denver, this region contains more than 1,000 species of plants and is primarily an area for study of the alpine tundra. For the novice hiker with only a casual interest in botany this trail offers stunning panoramas of the several snow-capped peaks and gnarled old trees that were whipped into weird and fanciful shapes by high altitude winds. Up here the possibilities for the artist or serious photographer are nearly endless.

To reach the trailhead, drive southwest from either Bergen Park or up from Idaho Springs on State Highway 103. At Echo Lake take State Highway 5, the Mount Evans Highway, to the marked trailhead. Incidentally, the Mount Evans road is the highest automobile road in North America and in good weather it may be driven all the way to the summit of 14,264 foot Mount Evans, a handsome peak that honors Dr. John Evans, Colorado's second Territorial Governor.

Park in the designated area at the trailhead. Usually there are printed guides to the trail in the box where the path begins. You will walk generally southwest. This is a trail for the nature lover, a route to be walked slowly not only because of the altitude but for the information to be gleaned as well. The walking distance is a modest two miles. Bring your camera and a lunch. Due to the elevation which limits plant growth, late summer or early autumn are the best seasons for this unusual hike.

Hikers enjoy a walk on the Pesman Trail.

At the high point on the Pesman Trail we can view the
Continental Divide.

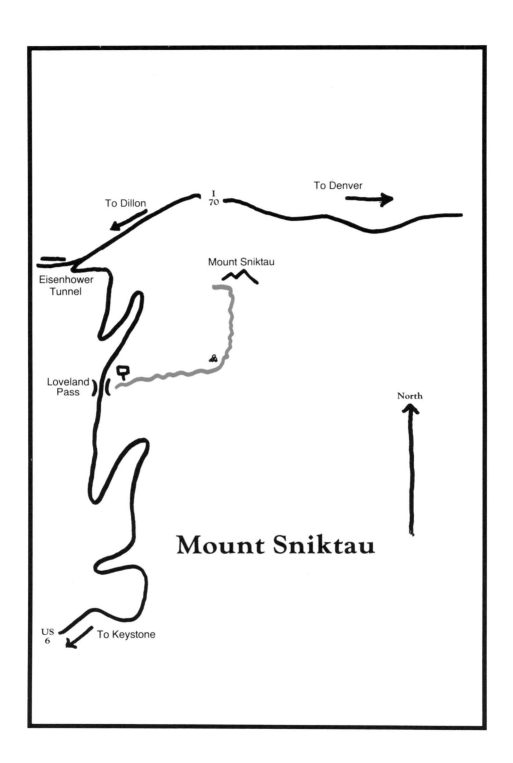

To Denver

To Dillon

I
70

Mount Sniktau

Eisenhower
Tunnel

Loveland
Pass

North

Mount Sniktau

US
6

To Keystone

MOUNT SNIKTAU

Mount Sniktau is a 13,235 foot high peak that is located barely to the east of the Continental Divide near Loveland Pass. Two versions persist concerning the origin of its name. The first is that it is an Indian word meaning "he who runs away fast." The other is that Sniktau was the nickname given to E.H.N. Patterson who succeeded Edward O. Wolcott as editor of the *Georgetown Miner* between 1873 and 1880. Although the peak cannot be seen from nearby Georgetown, it looms up prominently on the horizon as you approach the freeway overpass just west of Silver Plume.

This hike has always seemed to us to impart more of a special feeling of climbing in Colorado's Rockies and of a closeness to the mountains than most other easy climbs. Moreover, it is close to the Denver metropolitan area and is very easy to reach. From wherever you choose to start, drive to the top of Loveland Pass and park in the space provided on the east side of the road. At this writing a wooden sign indicates the start of the trail to Sniktau. Because this entire hike is above timberline you should check weather conditions carefully. Under no circumstances should you start up the ridge unless it is a clear day. Additionally, this area is frequently buffeted by moderately strong winds, so be sure to carry insulated clothing.

For the first mile beyond the trailhead the terrain is a bit steep. In fact it gains some 1200 feet of elevation during the first mile. Take your time and stop for a rest whenever it seems appropriate. When you have attained the ridge top turn left or north by the large rock cairn and walk along the saddle toward the two low, rounded mountains to the north. After crossing these summits you will see a narrow ridge slightly below you. Follow the path down and across the ridge. The east portal of the Eisenhower Tunnel can now be seen in the valley far below you.

Since this ridge and the next slope are strewn with large boulders, step carefully on the uphill side of the rocks. If they should roll, you will fall toward the mountain, which is less serious. From this point the sharply pointed summit that looms up to the north is Mount Sniktau. With no trail, merely pick your own route to the summit. Once you are on the top, turn in any direction and enjoy a superb view.

Behind you in the far southwest are the Maroon Peaks and the neighboring peaks near Aspen. Just to the north of them are the high summits of the Saguache Range, Mount of the Holy Cross, and the whole expanse of the Gore Range. Looking further north most of the Indian Peaks area can be seen extending nearly to Longs Peak. Fourteen thousand, two hundred and sixty seven foot high Torreys Peak is the closest mountain to the east. Fourteen thousand, two hundred and seventy foot Grays Peak peeks out from behind the top of Torreys. To the right or southeast are Grizzly Peak and the obscure Grizzly Pass. In the far distance to the east the jagged crest of Mount Evans can be seen while Squaw and Chief Mountains appear blue in the distance to the north of Evans. Be sure to carry binoculars, a camera, and color film with you on this hike.

When you are ready to return, simply retrace your route. If you prefer not to regain all of that elevation again, lateral around the west ridge of the two peaks after you have crossed the saddle. Be very careful not to descend the first ridge. Wait until you can see the summit of Loveland Pass below you, then start down. Once you have the trail in sight follow it down and you will soon reach your car. Total walking distance is about five miles.

For Mount Sniktau, our preferred seasons are mid-summer through autumn, or until the first threat of snow.

140

The massive peak at the right is Mount Sniktau.

From Sniktau's summit, Interstate 70 and the east portal of the
Eisenhower Tunnel are seen in the valley far below.

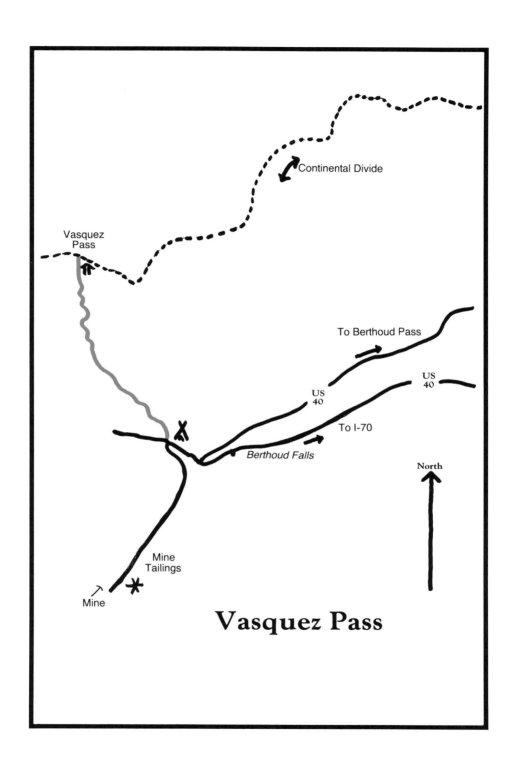

Continental Divide

Vasquez
Pass

To Berthoud Pass

US
40

US
40

To I-70

Berthoud Falls

North

Mine
Tailings

Mine

Vasquez Pass

VASQUEZ PASS

Vasquez Pass is an 11,655 foot high crossing of the Continental Divide, located between Vasquez Peak and Stanley Mountain. Historically, this crossing dates far back into Colorado's fur trade era in the nineteenth century. At one time Vasquez Pass almost made it as a primary wagon road across the range. It was named for Louis Vasquez, a mountain man who pioneered it as a means of tending his trap lines on opposite sides of the divide. Since most of these early traders rarely saw their names in print he was referred to as "Vaskiss" in several of the old fur company records.

Vasquez was a one time partner of Jim Bridger. Coutant's *History of Wyoming* states that Vasquez established a trading post in 1832 on Clear Creek, which was then called the Vasquez Fork. Robert L. Perkins' book *The First Hundred Years* describes the Vasquez fort as a stockade of logs and adobe located on the South Platte River five miles northeast of Denver on a high bluff and opposite the point where the Vasquez Fork empties into the South Platte River. The site is now occupied by a Public Service Company of Colorado transformer station.

Vasquez called his post Fort Convenience. From it he sent numerous expeditions up the creek and across Vasquez Pass to Old Park, the trapper's name for our Middle Park. His trading route took him up into Wyoming for trade with the Indians. Vasquez also built a cabin near Georgetown in 1832. It stood just west of the Berthoud Pass junction, on Clear Creek at the mouth of West Clear Creek.

Five years later, in 1837, he abandoned Fort Convenience and built the larger, better known and more permanent Fort Vasquez. Now reconstructed of adobe, it stands at the south edge of Platteville. Presumably, Vasquez continued to use his pass from the newer fort, although few historical references can be found for his activities in the 1840s and 1850s.

Then in 1862, William H. Russell of the firm of Russell, Majors and Waddell, entered into a partnership with William H. Byers. Byers was the founder of Colorado's oldest newspaper, the *Rocky Mountain News*. Together they hoped to push a wagon road through Vasquez Pass. Surprisingly, they nearly reached the top before the project was abandoned. Since that time no serious effort has been made to complete the road and the crossing remains as an obscure path today.

To get to Vasquez Pass take Interstate 70 west from Denver to the Empire–Berthoud Pass exit, which is US 40. At the west end of Berthoud Falls the road makes an abrupt switchback to the right. Here a second road marked Henderson Mine branches off to the left. Follow this left fork past the Big Bend campground. Park beside the Highway Department's green metal building above the right side of the road. Face the gasoline drums at the edge of the parking area and look directly above toward the wooded saddle. The Vasquez Pass trail goes through this saddle.

The actual trail is unmarked, steep, and difficult to locate. Begin walking straight up the hill from the gasoline drums toward the saddle. Here and there you will find signs of the path. About half way up the hill it curves left toward the stream but does not cross it. Instead, it parallels the flow, still climbing steeply. There is much downed timber to be crawled over and there are several switchbacks.

Beyond the saddle the trail leaves the trees and enters a pretty meadow filled with lovely wild flowers. In general the trail follows the right side of the meadow and is not far above the creek. Continue climbing and walk north toward the above timberline saddle at the head of the meadow. Here and there you will encounter fairly distinct sections of the trail, but nothing that resembles a wagon road. Most of the time you just keep walking to the north, carefully noting your surroundings as you go.

144

At right of center, the dim trail leading up to Vasquez Pass
can be seen.

Looking east is the panorama from the summit of Vasquez Pass.

Just beyond the saddle the path switches back through alpine vegetation to the summit of the pass.

On the top, the path is quite visible as it traverses the low swale. Beyond it in the distance is Middle Park. Presumably the trail follows Vasquez Creek down into the park, although we have not hiked it beyond the top. The round trip walking distance as described is just under six miles, with a 1200 foot elevation gain in the first three. Above all watch where you are going and carefully note appropriate landmarks in order to assure the return to your car without losing the way. Late summer and early fall are the best seasons for this hike. Be sure to carry your camera.

Vasquez Pass (elevation 11,655) crosses the Continental Divide through the low point on the horizon.

Watrous Gulch

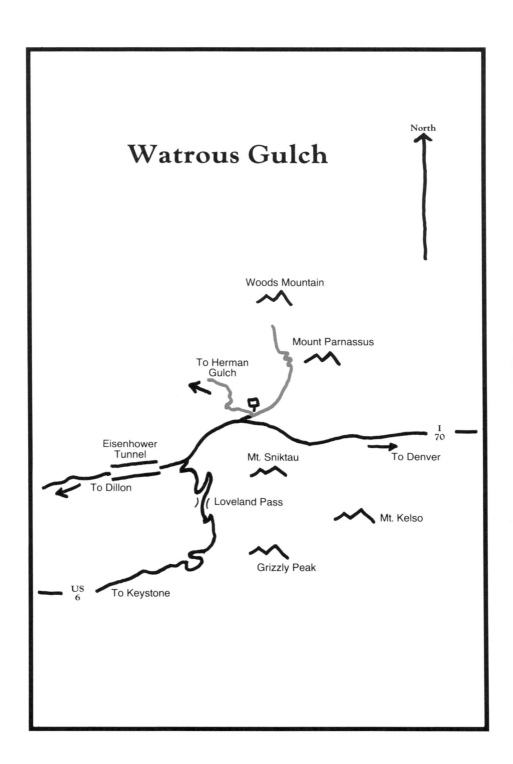

North

Woods Mountain

Mount Parnassus

To Herman
Gulch

Eisenhower
Tunnel

To Dillon

Mt. Sniktau

)(Loveland Pass

Mt. Kelso

Grizzly Peak

I
70

To Denver

US
6

To Keystone

WATROUS GULCH

Although the Watrous Gulch trail is a very pretty one, it is not a particularly well-known one. The trail is well-defined and is reasonably close to the Denver metropolitan area. Watrous Gulch offers natural shelter from storms, protection from the sun, and impressive views of several large mountains. But unfortunately it is not shown on the most recent Forest Service maps.

To reach the trailhead drive west from Denver on Interstate 70 through Idaho Springs, past Georgetown and Silver Plume. Watch for the Bakerville interchange but do not exit there. Continue on to the next exit which has neither a name nor a number at this writing. If you miss it and come to the Loveland Pass exit, turn around and go back to the first place where you can get off. Exit and park on the north side of the highway and facing a long gravel pile. Cross the ridge of gravel but do not go up the steep road to the north. Instead, take the old abandoned road back toward the east, paralleling the Interstate. Walk about an eighth of a mile to a brown Forest Service sign containing the names Watrous Gulch and Herman Gulch. Turn left here and walk uphill for an additional eighth of a mile to an old road that crosses the foot trail. Now turn right for about thirty feet and you will see the trail to Watrous Gulch.

For most of the first two miles the path is shrouded among big evergreen trees. Here and there you will encounter signs of deliberate trail building, grading, and rock cribbing. On the uphill side you may notice evidence of some older trail building, dim but still evident. We have been unable to find out who it was that built these pretty foot paths. Perhaps they antedate the Arapaho National Forest. In season the mushroom growth here is profuse. The area is moist, mostly in deep shade and is carpeted with many years' accumulation of decayed pine needles. In short, ideal conditions for a desirable mushroom culture. Needless to say, one should exercise care when picking mushrooms. Many wild mushrooms are unsafe to eat while others are poisonous. If in doubt leave them alone.

Gradually the path contours around the east side of the mountain, heading toward the northwest. It becomes moderately steep until it breaks out into a near timberline meadow. Notice the evidence of an old forest fire on the mountainside above and to the east of the trail. Another half mile or so will take you close to the stream that flows down from the Continental Divide. The remains of what was probably a sawmill can be seen beside the fast moving water. On the opposite side of the stream a second foot path is visible. It contours along above water level for some distance but we have never followed it.

Our path is the more distinct one, moving less steeply uphill from this point and away from the stream. Suddenly the path stops, but there are rock cairns to mark the way if you care to continue on up into the basin. A dense undergrowth of willows makes following the trail more difficult. If you want to stay on the trail be sure to get each succeeding cairn in sight before leaving the preceding one. There should be no problem if you lose the trail so long as you stay within the valley. The cairns merely indicate some other person's choice of the easiest way through the willows. Becoming lost in this valley would require great dedication to that principle.

The round trip distance up to the point where the cairns stop and the return to the trailhead is about five miles. Continuing up to the head of the valley will add another couple of miles. The prominent mountains to the south are Kelso and Grizzly peaks. To the left of them, just before you drop down into the trees on your return, you can see the long ridge of Mount McClellan. The abrupt cleft on its ridge is the place where America's highest operating railroad, the Argentine Central, reached its apex.

The Watrous Gulch path can be seen at the lower left in this picture.

Most of the Watrous Gulch Trail lies in a heavily wooded area.

We have sometimes been able to hike the Watrous Gulch trail until late November. The thick tree growth seems to keep the trail in passable condition. Late spring, summer, and autumn are preferable. Those large trees also offer shelter and some desirable picnic spots with a view. In season, expect to find a variety of pretty wild flowers up here, adding touches of color to the attractive mountain panorama.

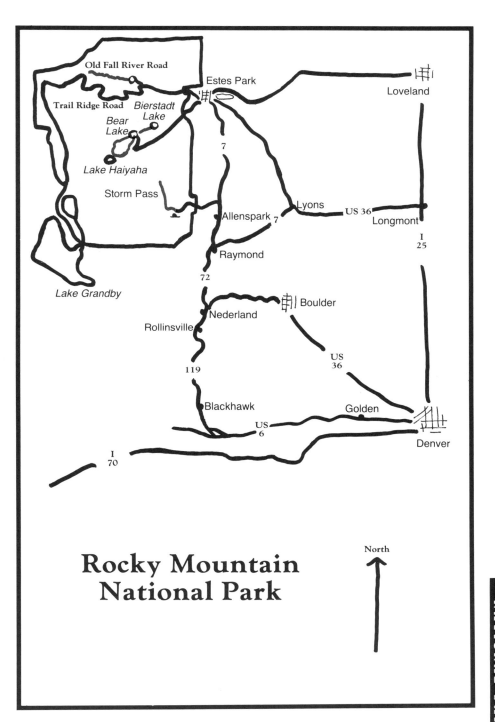

Old Fall River Road

Trail Ridge Road

Bierstadt
Lake

Bear
Lake

Lake Haiyaha

Storm Pass

Lake Grandby

Estes Park

Loveland

7

Lyons

US 36

Longmont

I
25

Allenspark 7

Raymond

72

Nederland

Boulder

Rollinsville

US
36

119

Blackhawk

Golden

US
6

Denver

I
70

North

Rocky Mountain
National Park

Trail Ridge Road

Emerald Lake   Nymph Lake   Bear Lake
Dream Lake

Lake Haiyaha

Glacier
Gorge

Alberta Falls -
Haiyaha Circle

Longs Peak

North

To
Allenspark

36

Estes
Park

7

THE ALBERTA FALLS
LAKE HAIYAHA CIRCLE

Rocky Mountain National Park is a glorious place for the hiker and nature lover. To reach the park drive north from Denver on Interstate 25. Exit at the Lyons ramp, continue through Lyons to Estes Park and the park entrance.

Here is a colorful autumn hike to be enjoyed within Rocky Mountain National Park. In fact, it is a pretty walk for any season except winter. Begin by driving to the parking lot for Bear Lake. The trail starts just behind the information booth. Turn abruptly to your left immediately beyond the booth and follow the well-landscaped trail southeast, downhill to Glacier Gorge Junction. Here the path turns south, paralleling Glacier Creek upward toward Alberta Falls. This impressive cataract was named for Alberta Sprague, wife of Abner Sprague, an early day homesteader within the present area of the park. Sprague Lake likewise honors the family name.

Above the falls the trail climbs moderately upward through groves of deciduous and evergreen trees. Generally this is a shaded and well-protected trail. Just before it reaches Lake Haiyaha, it enters a boulder field of tremendous proportions. Huge granite slabs all but bar access to the lake. One must literally climb or crawl over nearly a quarter of a mile of this natural obstacle course to reach the shore of this rather attractive body of water. Anyway, as a lunch shop you will find rocks of every size and shape to accommodate even the most discriminating sitting posture.

As you leave, watch for the trail junction just a few yards down the path. Go left or north at this point. When you come to breaks in between the trees, look off

A handsome panorama can be found along the well-marked Lake Haiyaha Trail.

This lovely waterfall is just one of the views you may enjoy while hiking the Lake Haiyaha Trail.

to the right for several impressive views of Longs Peak. Further down, the trail skirts a small pond and intersects another trail, the much used right-of-way from Bear Lake to Emerald Lake. The trails intersect between Dream and Nymph Lakes. Turn right or east here and return to the parking lot at Bear Lake. We feel that summer and autumn are the preferred times for this hike.

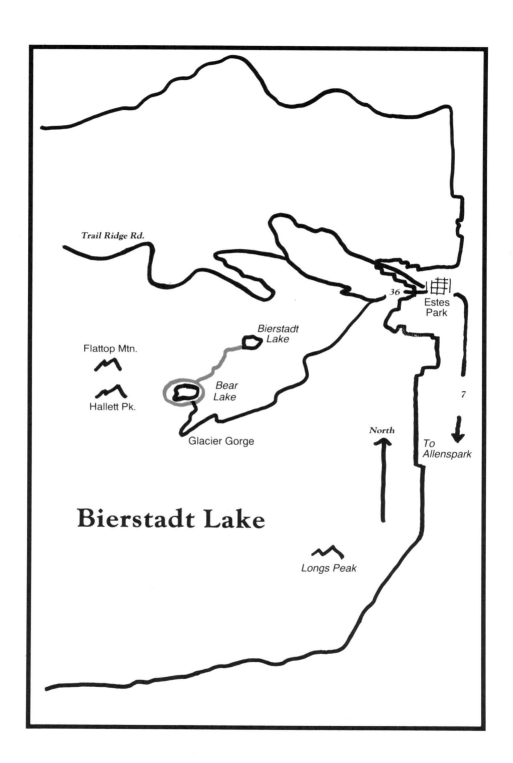

Trail Ridge Rd.

36

Estes
Park

Bierstadt
Lake

Flattop Mtn.

Bear
Lake

Hallett Pk.

7

Glacier Gorge

North

To
Allenspark

Bierstadt Lake

Longs Peak

BIERSTADT LAKE

Albert Bierstadt was a native of Germany. Born in 1830, he lived a full life, passing away in 1902. In the interim years he traveled widely in the western part of the United States. Bierstadt supported himself by painting huge canvases of the landscapes that he loved. Several of his paintings depict panoramas that he had seen and enjoyed in the Estes Park area. One such scene, a large and colorful nineteenth century painting in oils, shows Longs Peak. It now hangs in the Western History Department on the fourth floor of the Denver Public Library. So it is entirely appropriate that one of the loveliest lakes in Rocky Mountain National Park should have been named in his memory.

To visit the park drive north from Denver on Interstate 25 to the Lyons exit, then west on US 36 to Estes Park village. Pick up a map as you enter Rocky Mountain National Park and drive to the Bear Lake parking lot. At the north end of the lot, beyond the rest rooms, a pretty trail circles Bear Lake. Walk to the right on this trail to the first junction where a sign will direct you to Bierstadt Lake. Turn right at this point and begin walking toward the northeast.

This is a broad, well-landscaped trail, wooded and shady for the entire two miles to the lake. The few grades are quite modest and the changes in altitude, if any, will cause no discomfort. This is probably the most level trail in this book. In fact, you will lose slightly more altitude than you will gain. Bear Lake's altitude is 9,475 feet while that of Bierstadt is a mere 9,416. Primarily, this hike is more of a leisurely stroll than a climb.

Upon arriving at the lake you experience a truly breathtaking view of the snowy peaks that provide a backdrop to this lovely spot. To the West you will see Flattop Mountain, 12,725 foot Hallett Peak and Otis Peak, among others. There is a little path that goes to the left from the point where the main trail arrives at the lake. In June we have enjoyed seeing ducks and their young along the shore, very close to the path. There are other paths in the vicinity of the lake. Most lead to secluded picnic spots, all of which afford good views of the nearby mountains.

Your return to Bear Lake follows the same route, although there is a longer alternative that leaves the main path a short distance from the lake. It goes off to the right or west and loses and gains altitude several times before rejoining the original trail near Bear Lake. The round trip distance to and from Bierstadt Lake is just four miles, or five if you choose to return by the longer route.

Although we have heard of people making this trek on snowshoes in winter, we have not tried it ourselves. Summer and autumn are the seasons that we have preferred for this walk, but whenever you go, be sure to carry a camera.

Looking across Bierstadt Lake, Hallett Peak is the mountain in the center of the picture.

A mother duck and her young swim without fear at the edge of Bierstadt Lake.

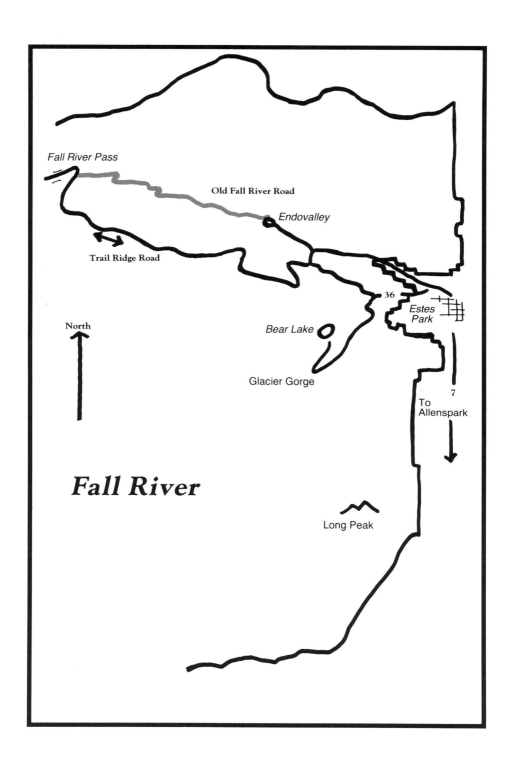

Fall River Pass

Old Fall River Road

Endovalley

Trail Ridge Road

36

Estes Park

North

Bear Lake

Glacier Gorge

7

To
Allenspark

Fall River

Long Peak

162

FALL RIVER ROAD

Colorado has two Fall Rivers. The first is located barely west of Idaho Springs. The other one is the subject of this chapter. It is an old trail that is located in Rocky Mountain National Park. As the name suggests, it is named for a river. Fall River rises on the Continental Divide south of 11,796 foot high Fall River Pass. It flows southeast through Estes Park village and into Lake Estes. Paralleling the river and north of it the Fall River Road climbs up to the northwest from US 34. The road is steep, narrow in places, and historic. Before Trail Ridge Road was built, the Fall River Road was the prime route into the park's high country. It was never paved and is closed to motorized traffic after Labor Day and through the winter. During this off season, it becomes a fine hiking trail and snowshoe route.

You should enter Rocky Mountain National Park at the Fall River entrance, five miles northwest of Estes Park. Continue on for two miles to the junction. Do not turn left, go on toward Endovalley Campground. Do not enter the campground. Park near the barricade and begin hiking up the old Fall River Road. Depending on available time and the weather, this hike can be tailored to most any need. From the starting point the road continues upward for nine miles to the summit of Fall River Pass, where it connects with Trail Ridge Road.

Because it is old and narrow it is used only as a one way, downhill only road during the "people season." As a hiking path it is easy to follow and there is no chance of becoming lost. Most of the road lies in growths of evergreen timber, with ample opportunities to observe the lovely mountain panoramas. However, the upper reaches get up above timberline and afford magnificent vistas of the big peaks that surround Fall River Pass.

Rocky Mountain NATIONAL PARK

Start here when hiking the Fall River Road.

The beauty of Rocky Mountain National Park may be enjoyed on a
hike along the Fall River Road.

In summer there is also the possibility of a two car downhill hike. Leave one car at the lower trailhead just described. Drive the other with all hikers up Trail Ridge Road to the top of the pass and leave the second car at that point. Now hike the scenic and easy nine miles downhill to the first automobile, then drive up to retrieve the other car. In summer you may share the right-of-way with a few cars that choose this unpaved route. In autumn, before Trail Ridge Road is closed, the use of two cars in a very attractive alternative.

So there are at least two possibilities for this historic route. Our preferences are autumn for walking and winter for snowshoeing.

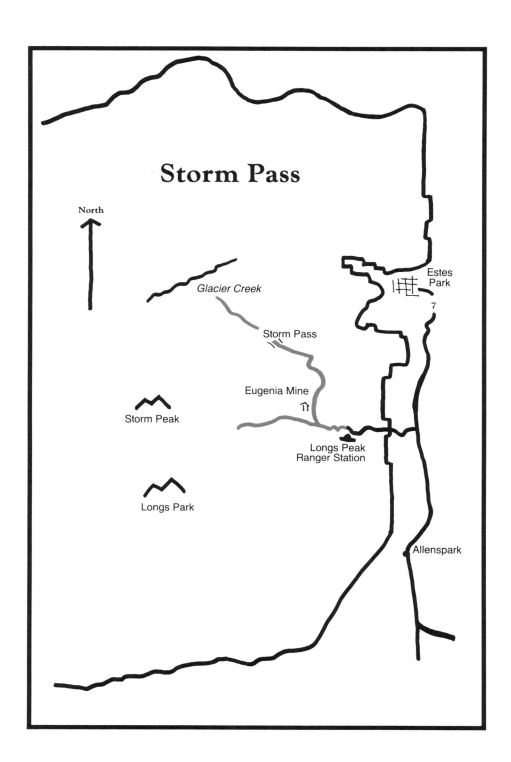

Storm Pass

North

Glacier Creek

Storm Pass

Eugenia Mine

Storm Peak

Longs Park

Longs Peak
Ranger Station

Estes
Park

7

Allenspark

STORM PASS

Storm Pass has never been anything except a hiking path. It is one of those not too well-known crossings of the smaller range to the east of the Continental Divide in Rocky Mountain National Park. Its crest is within the modest 10,000 foot altitude range. It is an easy walk to the top. The late Louisa Ward Arps told us that both Storm Pass and nearby Storm Peak were named by the naturalist Enos Mills who considered them a gathering place for inclement weather.

Colorado State Highway 7 runs north and south, paralleling the eastern boundary of Rocky Mountain National Park. South of Estes Park village you should turn off to the west and drive to the parking area for the Longs Peak Ranger Station. Begin walking on the marked trail leading to Longs Peak itself. Along the way you will see the ruined cabins of the Eugenia Mine, a precious metal location that dates back to the era prior to the park's establishment.

Where the trail forks, go to the right and continue climbing up to the pass. Virtually all of this trail lies within a dense growth of evergreens, offering shade for most of the distance. Consequently there are few viewpoints from which one may look out to enjoy the surrounding mountain panoramas.

If you should choose to continue on across the pass it will take you down to the popular Glacier Creek Trail, making for a total walking distance of just over five miles. From the Longs Peak Ranger Station to the top, the distance is barely over two miles and less than five miles for the round trip. Summer and autumn are our preferred seasons for the walk to Storm Pass.

Hikers enjoy the well-laid out trail to Storm Pass.

The end of Storm Pass Trail.

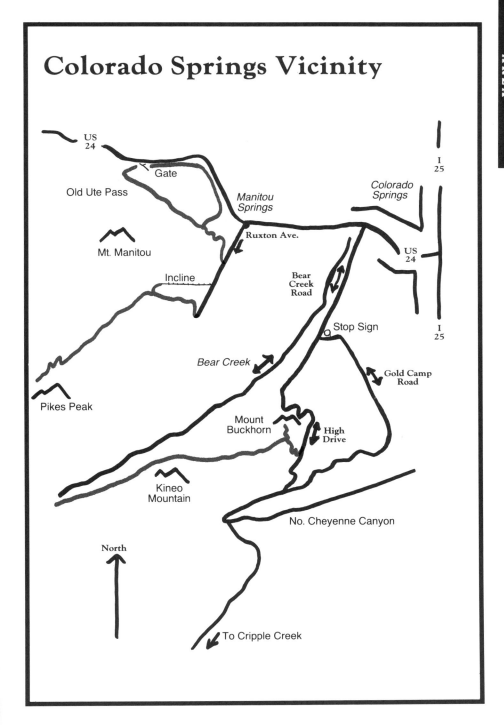

Colorado Springs Vicinity

US 24

Gate

Old Ute Pass

Manitou Springs

Colorado Springs

I 25

Mt. Manitou

Ruxton Ave.

US 24

Incline

Bear Creek Road

Stop Sign

I 25

Bear Creek

Gold Camp Road

Pikes Peak

Mount Buckhorn

High Drive

Kineo Mountain

No. Cheyenne Canyon

North

To Cripple Creek

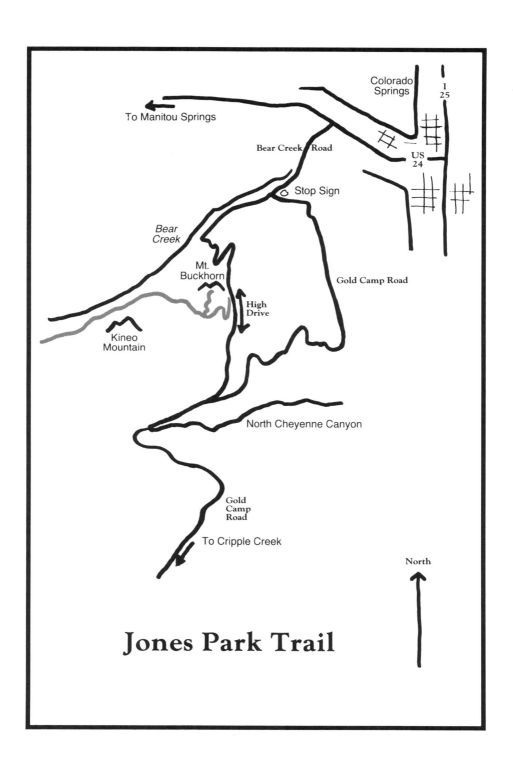

Jones Park Trail

JONES PARK

This is only one of the many interesting hikes that originate in the Pikes Peak area. To reach the trailhead, leave Interstate 25 at the Manitou Springs exit on the south side of Colorado Springs. Drive west on US 24 to the 26th Street exit and turn left or south. Continue south on the Bear Creek road to a stop sign. Turn abruptly left here and follow the road that runs sharply uphill to the southeast. You are now following the abandoned grade of the Colorado Springs and Cripple Creek Railway, now known as the Gold Camp Road. President Theodore Roosevelt once rode the train over this grade up to Cripple Creek. He described the scenery as "bankrupting the English language."

This unpaved road passes through two old tunnels and goes through the original railroad cuts. Pause when you reach the parking area at the start of the High Drive. At this point the road ahead traverses a lovely drive of just over thirty miles to the Victor–Cripple Creek area. The turn to the left goes back to Colorado Springs through scenic North Cheyenne Canyon. In autumn this is a very pretty area. Of the several roads mentioned, the one you want is the High Drive. Sometimes the Colorado Springs Parks Department locks the gate at the High Drive after October 1st, so check before driving up here. If the gate is open drive up to the parking area at the top of the High Drive and leave the car at this point. Otherwise, go around the gate and walk just over a mile up the graded road to this point. Now cross the road to the rock wall that carries the inscription "High Drive, Altitude 7,867, C.W.C. '34."

The steps at either end of the wall will take you to the start of the trail. Avoid the path that leads uphill. Follow the one that parallels the road you followed up here. The

All of the trail to Jones Park is scenic.

Evelyn Brown poses at a turn on the trail up to Jones Park.

path gains altitude quickly and you soon lose sight of the road. In dry weather this can be a rather dusty trail. Its base is the native soil with crushed rocks added. Where the trail bends to the right around the southern shoulder of Mount Buckhorn, a second path turns uphill to the north and goes to the summit of Buckhorn, a pleasant picnic spot. At this point you are just under two miles from your destination.

The Jones Park trail traverses around the west side of Mount Buckhorn, then angles north for a short distance. Next it turns generally west along the north slope of Kineo Mountain, following Bear Canyon to 9,000 foot high Jones Park. The round trip distance for this hike is about six miles. Add two more if that gate at the trailhead is locked. You will gain approximately 1,200 feet of elevation as you come up. Summer and autumn, before October 1st, are the times we prefer for this hike.

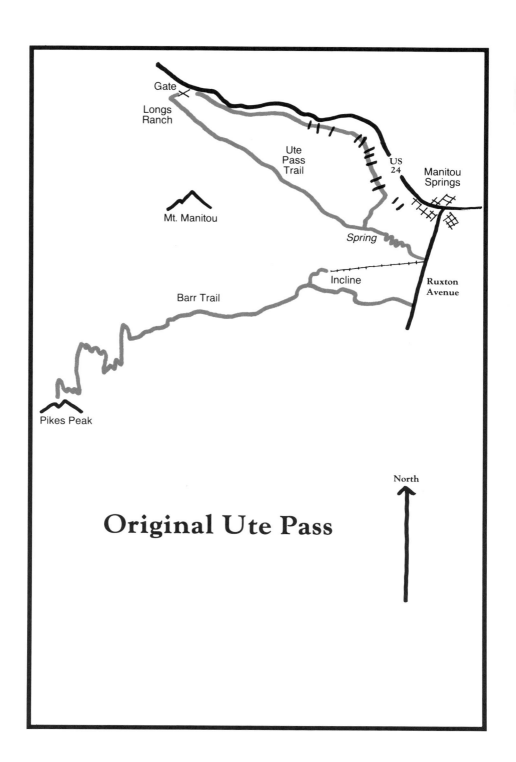

Gate

Longs
Ranch

Ute
Pass
Trail

US
24

Manitou
Springs

Mt. Manitou

Spring

Incline

Ruxton
Avenue

Barr Trail

Pikes Peak

North

Original Ute Pass

THE ORIGINAL UTE PASS

Before taking this hike, please read this chapter through in its entirety. If you decide to go, take a stout rope and a flashlight with you.

Colorado's historic 6,800 foot high Ute Pass is paved now and is shown on contemporary maps as US Highway 24. It runs generally northwest from Manitou Springs. Perhaps because of its low summit it was once a foot trail that provided easy access for the Ute people who wanted to visit their kinsmen in South Park. But today's US 24 is not the original route to the pass. The earlier trail lies roughly a half mile to the south in the next canyon. It is with this earlier, unimproved original trail that this chapter will be concerned.

If you approach the area by Interstate 25, as most people do, leave the freeway at the Manitou Springs exit. Drive through the town to Ruxton Avenue, near the western extremity of Manitou Springs. Turn left or south on Ruxton to the parking area for the Mount Manitou Incline. After parking, begin walking along the graded road that passes the lower end of the structure that houses the ticketseller and the restrooms. Walk along this road for a short way to Rattlesnake Gulch. Here the trail runs briefly downhill to the northwest. You are now on the original Indian path.

For this first half mile or so to the top of the first summit you will encounter the steepest grades of the whole trail. Stop and rest often, the Utes probably did. Time as we perceive it meant little to our original people since they had nothing better to do than play Indian all day anyway. At the top of the first hill a refreshingly cool spring flows from the hillside on the right side of the trail in early summer. Although we have never suffered any ill effects from drinking its water, anything can happen to a fresh mountain spring and the use of chlorine tablets would probably be advisable.

In the early days this steep pitch up from the Springs of Manitou was known as "Paper Collar Canyon" for the abundant number of those expendable accoutrements of proper male attired that were discarded beside the trail by sweaty tourists. When paper collars went out of style, the name was changed to Rattlesnake Gulch or Canyon for reasons that we shudder to consider.

At this point the trail drops down, losing perhaps a third of the elevation gained thus far. The lost elevation is regained once more as you make your way up to the top of summit number two. By this time it should be apparent to you why this route did not remain as the primary wagon road to Ute Pass.

As the trail drops downhill once more, watch for the scars and the sign indicating the point at which the wagon road joined the older Ute foot path as it comes in from the right. From this point on the road and the trail were one and the same. Some chronology and a few facts might be of interest at this point.

Prior to the gold rush of 1859–60 this entire route was, as the name would indicate, only an Indian foot path. Then in 1860 placer gold was found in California Gulch, adjacent to contemporary Leadville. Since present roads to Lake County did not exist at that time, gold seekers came south from Cherry Creek to old Colorado City, between Manitou and Colorado Springs. Next they followed Fountain Creek for a short distance to the side gulch that led them to the Ute Trail. After crossing Ute, Wilkerson, and Trout Creek Passes to the Arkansas Valley, they followed the east side of the river to California Gulch.

This is the same route followed by Augusta and H.A.W. Tabor and hundreds of others. Mrs. Tabor's diary tells how they built up the grades here and there in order to get their wagon through. Some days, she noted, they progressed less than five miles. At night they could look back down on their previous evening's campsite. Two weeks were required for travel from the plains to South Park. Colorado City put a work force into the

Both a downgrade and one of the upgrades can be seen in this picture
of the original Ute Pass Trail.

Hikers approach the railroad tunnel on the return trip from Ute Pass,
US Highway 24 lies in the valley at the left.

177

gulch in June of 1860 to build and improve the road. It continued in use until 1872, when the present Ute Pass was completed.

Meanwhile, back on the trail, at the point where the wagon road merged with the foot path, a glance ahead will reveal a third hill to be ascended. Beyond it are summits four and five. Next you will come to a dilapidated homestead on your right. It was called Long's Ranch. At this altitude Mr. Long's lilacs, long abandoned, still bloom in early June. We like this as a lunch stop and perhaps a good place to re-think your objectives. From here on, the old trail is difficult to find. If the weather is warm, as it often is in this canyon, it may seem that you have walked more than the slightly generous three miles actually traversed to this point. This being the case, Long's Ranch is a good place to turn back and follow the trail down to your car.

But if you are "adventuresome," and have a really good eye for following rather obscure trails, a rope, and flashlight, there is an alternative way back. Frankly, it is not for everyone. Instead of continuing on the regular path back down, turn east on Mr. Long's wagon road and walk just over a half mile to US 24. Climb over or through the large metal gate and walk ever so carefully for a half mile beside zooming cars to the point where James Hagerman's Colorado Midland railroad grade can be seen on the right. Here the most sure footed member of the party should take one end of the rope and cross the embankment to the railroad grade. This can be a treacherous spot and you should think about it before you go on. You could walk on down the road to Manitou Springs.

If you elect the railroad grade you will hike downhill through five tunnels. One of them has a curved interior, making it dark inside. Here is the place where you will need that flashlight. Do not enter tunnel six as it exits onto private land and is barricaded. Instead, head up the gulch to your right. Here the path is very dim in some places so be especially watchful. At one point there is a steep shelf of slippery rock where you may be more comfortable using that rope again. This is not a great trail, even though wheeled vehicles are alleged to have used it a century or more ago.

Where this path intersects the Ute Trail again you should turn left. You still need to re-cross summits one and two again before reaching your car. At this point you have walked in the neighborhood of seven miles. The best seasons for the Ute Trail are late spring (but watch for ticks), summer, and autumn.

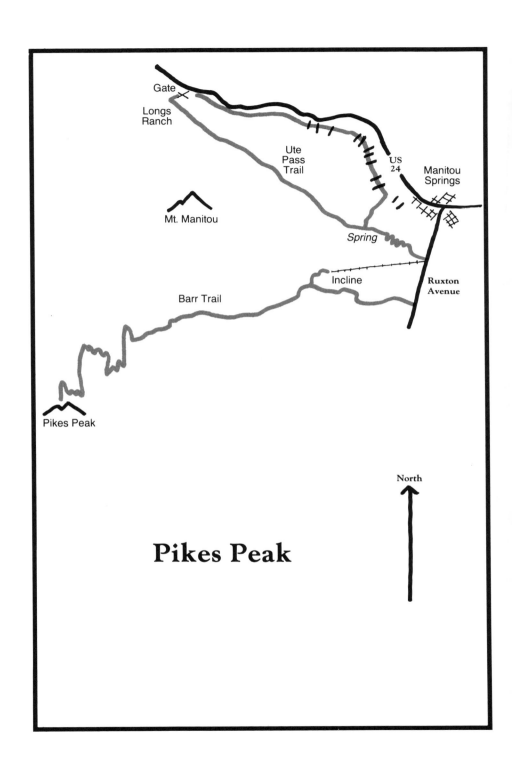

Gate

Longs
Ranch

Ute
Pass
Trail

US
24

Manitou
Springs

Mt. Manitou

Spring

Incline

Ruxton
Avenue

Barr Trail

Pikes Peak

North

Pikes Peak

PIKES PEAK

Many published sources have referred to Pikes Peak as "America's most famous mountain." Lieutenant Zebulon Pike used it as a landmark, a convenient reference point, in 1806. Also, he tried but failed to climb it in November of that year. This ill-starred attempt make Pike forever famous as the first American who never climbed Pikes Peak. Dr. Edwin James, physician and botanist with the 1820 expedition of Major Stephen H. Long, was the first person known to have reached its broad summit. Pike probably "cliffed out" on Miller Mountain, but James and two friends stumbled upon the easier Ruxton Creek route and reached the top in July of 1820. They spent about an hour on the summit, enjoying the splendid view in all directions.

Although Major Long wanted to call the mountain James Peak in honor of the first ascent, the public never accepted it. Then came John C. Fremont's 1843 map. Fremont labeled it Pikes Peak and the dye was cast. Julia A. Holmes, early champion of women's rights, became the first of her sex to reach the top. Mrs. Holmes insisted that she could do anything a man could, and she proved it in 1858. Later she divorced her husband, who had followed her up the mountain and listened as she read Emerson's Essays during a snow flurry on the top. Julia moved to New Mexico where she became an ardent advocate of equality for ladies.

In the 1870s, the well-known Barr Trail was constructed up the slopes from Manitou Springs. It gains 7,500 feet of elevation in twelve miles. An annual foot race up Pikes Peak is conducted each year using the Barr Trail. In 1889 a wagon and carriage road was completed to the top, using still another approach. Pikes Peak came in for further public attention when Katharine Lee Bates,

Look north from the summit of Pikes Peak.

From the rock-strewn top of Pikes Peak, the Sangre de Cristo
Mountains can be seen.

182

a teacher from Massachusetts, expressed her feelings about the view from the summit in the lovely and still popular "America the Beautiful." Steepest and shortest of all the ways up the mountain is the Manitou and Pikes Peak Cog Railway. Its 8.9 mile track to the 14,110 foot elevation makes it the world's highest standard gauge railroad line.

So there are many ways to enjoy the exhilaration of standing on the rocky top of America's most famous mountain. Most of you who read this will doubtless prefer the hiking route. In Manitou Springs, Ruxton Avenue leads to the Cog Railway depot, then continues on for an additional half mile of access to a few homes. Where the street ends the Barr Trail begins. It is eleven and a half miles from this point to the top, or twelve miles from the depot. Although long, it is a nicely graded and well-defined path. Most hikers prefer doing Pikes Peak in two days. At 9,800 feet the original Barr Camp still provides the most used overnight shelter.

For the dedicated but less hardy hiker one additional alternative exists. This too begins at the depot on Ruxton Avenue. At the depot you may purchase a one way ticket on the popular Mount Manitou Incline. Ride this conveyance to the top of nearby Mount Manitou, enjoy the scenery and have lunch. Since the Barr Trail passes this point, hike it back down the easy two miles to the parking area. Summer and autumn would be the better months for Pikes Peak, by whatever means.

Among the rarest of the animals found in Colorado, the Rocky Mountain Goat can be viewed in several of the more remote above-timberline locations.

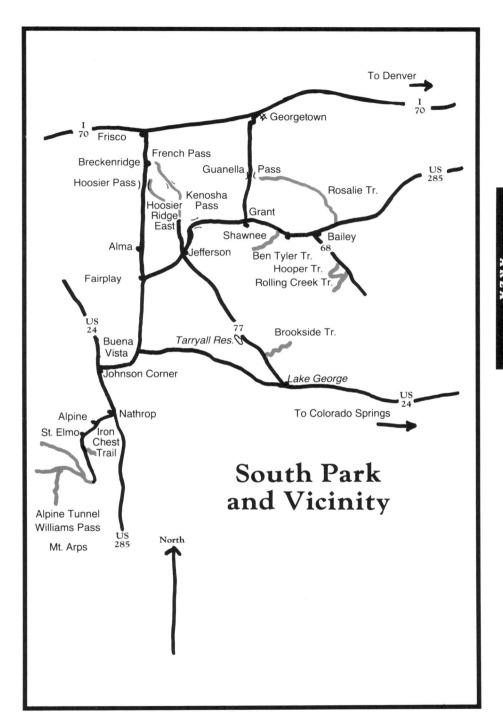

To Denver

I
70

I
70 Frisco

Georgetown

French Pass

Breckenridge

Guanella (Pass

US
285

Hoosier Pass)

Rosalie Tr.

Kenosha
Pass

Hoosier
Ridge
East

Grant

Shawnee

Bailey

Alma

Jefferson

Ben Tyler Tr.

68

Fairplay

Hooper Tr.

Rolling Creek Tr.

US
24

77

Brookside Tr.

Buena
Vista

Tarryall Res.

Johnson Corner

Lake George

Alpine

Nathrop

US
24

St. Elmo

Iron
Chest
Trail

To Colorado Springs

South Park
and Vicinity

Alpine Tunnel
Williams Pass

Mt. Arps

US
285

North

185

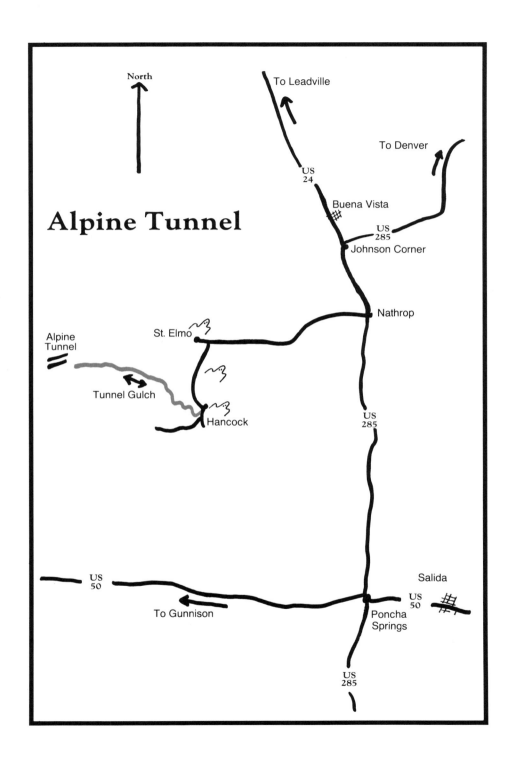

Alpine Tunnel

North

To Leadville

To Denver

US 24

Buena Vista

US 285

Johnson Corner

Nathrop

St. Elmo

Alpine Tunnel

Tunnel Gulch

Hancock

US 285

Salida

US 50

To Gunnison

US 50

Poncha Springs

US 285

ALPINE TUNNEL

Colorado's Alpine Tunnel is a most historic place. By 1878 the Denver, South Park, and Pacific Railroad had decided to enter the respective races to Gunnison and Leadville. It had already built up through Platte Canyon as far as Bailey. By 1880, its tracks had reached Nathrop, south of Buena Vista, on the way to Gunnison. That same year saw construction begun on the tunnel's 11,523 foot high bore. The necessary 500 feet through the mountain had been completed before the end of 1881. By tunneling under Alpine Pass, the railroad could save precious miles and avoid some of the hazards attendant upon operating a scheduled train over the Continental Divide in winter.

Skilled stonemasons were brought over from Italy to carve ornamental designs on the structures at the west end. Huge redwood timbers were imported from California to shore up the tunnel's roof. Unfortunately, lives were lost during construction. Surprisingly, the tunnel lasted for thirty years. A final train passed through it on November 10, 1910. With disuse it collapsed near the western end and both portals have now been closed for safety reasons.

On the western side you can drive all the way up to the portal if you are careful. In places a 4-wheel drive helps, but it is the eastern approach that we recommend for this hike. Drive south eight miles from Buena Vista on US 285. Turn west or right on County Road 162 at Nathrop. The pavement ends four miles west of Nathrop.

Continue along past the old town of Alpine, now a development of summer homes, to the ghost town of St. Elmo. At the eastern edge of the old town a dirt road takes off uphill to the southwest. At a point about two and a half miles up the road you will enter the town of

A gradual four per cent grade leads up to the east portal
of the Alpine Tunnel.

The old railroad ties have left horizontal scars on the abandoned grade
to the Alpine Tunnel.

188

Romley, whose buildings once stood below the road. A like distance beyond Romley will take you into Hancock, a long abandoned mining and railroad town. Leave your car at this point.

At Hancock there is a confusing choice of routes. If you go on straight ahead or south, the trail becomes a swampy route to Hancock Lake and Chalk Creek Pass. A branch trail turns off to the west and ascends the beautiful 4-wheel drive road to Hancock Pass. The trail we want swings abruptly to the right, crosses Chalk Creek via an old railroad bridge and proceeds northwest up Tunnel Gulch. You will be walking on a great abundance of old rotting railroad ties, so you can't mistake the route.

Because trains could climb only a four per cent grade, the trail is not steep. From Hancock to the buried east portal of the tunnel the distance is an easy three miles. In railroad days there was a small settlement just below the grade near the east portal. It was called Atlantic. If you have made prior transportation arrangements you can now continue north from the tunnel on a dim trail that parallels the Continental Divide for another four or five miles. Eventually it crosses the North Fork of Chalk Creek, intersecting the Tin Cup Pass trail. Turn right here and it is downhill all the way back to St. Elmo.

Any way you choose to approach it, the hike to Alpine Tunnel is a memorable one. Incidentally, the entire trail system lies within the San Isabel National Forest and is clearly shown on their map. Try this hike anytime between the end of June and the first snowfall.

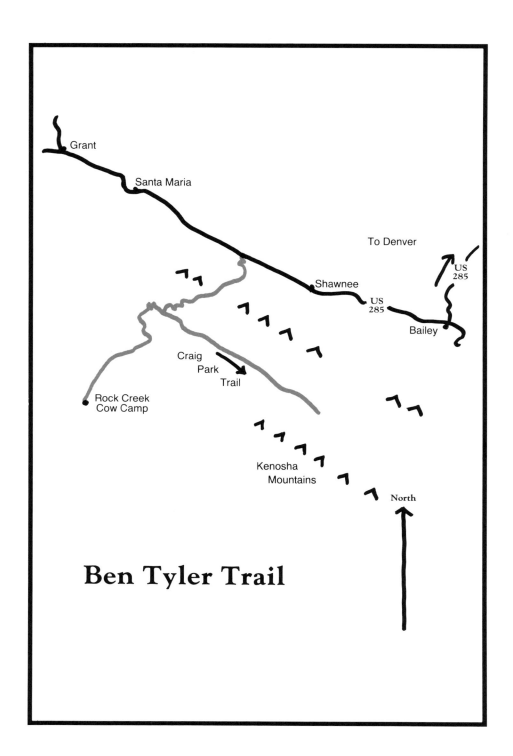

Grant

Santa Maria

To Denver

Shawnee

US
285

US
285

Bailey

Craig
Park
Trail

Rock Creek
Cow Camp

Kenosha
Mountains

North

Ben Tyler Trail

BEN TYLER TRAIL

This trail honors the memory of the Reverend Benjamin Tyler, a native of Illinois who was sent to Colorado in 1900. He served as pastor of the South Broadway Christian Church and was elected president of the International Sunday School Association in 1902.

To arrive at the trailhead for this interesting walk, drive west from Denver on US 285. Go on through Bailey and past Shawnee for one and a half miles. Watch carefully for the parking area on the right with a U.S. Forest Service sign. The sign identifies this as trail #606, the Ben Tyler Trail. Now we come to the most dangerous part of the hike, walking south across US 285! Walk diagonally toward the brown posts. The path starts from this point.

Within the first half mile, the trail traverses eleven abrupt switchbacks, most of which have guard rails. At the point of one sharp turn you will find a directional sign indicating that the Craig Park Trail is six miles away and that the Rock Creek Cow Camp may be reached in nine miles. A large gate across the trail should be closed after you have passed through it. Beyond the switchbacks the trail enters a broad meadow and continues climbing upward into a mixed grove of evergreen and deciduous trees. In general this is a sheltered trail, shady throughout most of its distance. It offers very few opportunities for viewing distant mountain panoramas. The forest is much too thick for scenery of that particular kind.

Within the first mile you will find an unnamed creek. The trail parallels it for some distance, crosses the stream on logs and rocks and continues climbing steeply upward. The groves of trees can only be described as handsome. At a distance of about four miles the path divides. The left fork goes downhill 1.2 miles to Craig

191

This is a typical section along the shaded Ben Tyler Trail.

During autumn, the lighter colored trees are some of the yellow aspens to be seen along the Ben Tyler Trail.

Meadows. Two more miles along the main trail will put you on the top of the ridge, affording a somewhat better view. One additional mile will bring you to the next trail junction. By this time you are on the western side of the ridge.

This is a fine but potentially dusty trail for a summer hike. However, autumn is our own preference. The narrow path above the creek where it traverses a steep hillside would probably rule this area out as a desirable snowshoe trail.

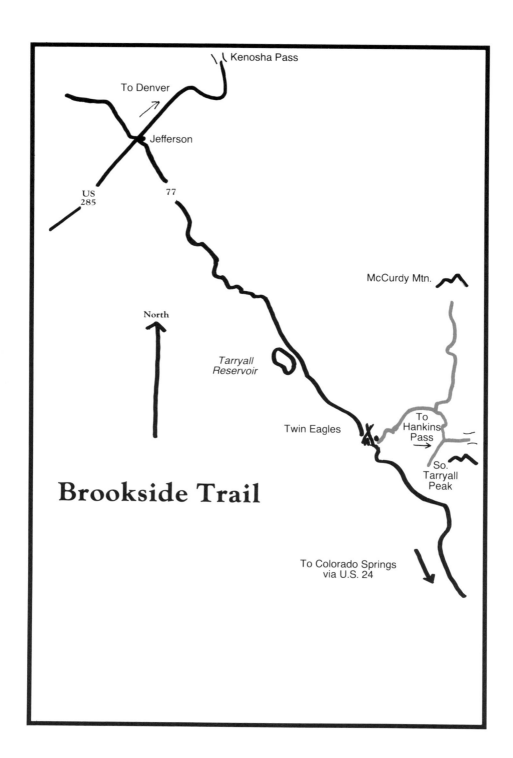

Kenosha Pass

To Denver

Jefferson

US
285

77

McCurdy Mtn.

North

Tarryall
Reservoir

To
Hankins
Pass

Twin Eagles

So.
Tarryall
Peak

Brookside Trail

To Colorado Springs
via U.S. 24

BROOKSIDE TRAIL

This entire hike lies within South Park and is a part of the trails system of the Pike National Forest. To find its trailhead take US 285 southwest out of Denver. Cross Kenosha Pass into South Park and continue on to the little town of Jefferson. Here you should turn southeast on County Road 77 toward Lake George. Primarily, this is a gravel-surfaced road, although some sections have been paved. You will pass the Rocky Canyon Picnic Ground and the Tarryall Reservoir. Beyond the reservoir watch for the Twin Eagles Picnic Ground on your left. Turn here and drive downhill to the parking lot. The trail begins here.

If you are approaching from Colorado Springs go west up Ute Pass, continue past Divide and Florissant on US 24. Just beyond the town of Lake George, turn right onto County Road 77 and drive northwest to the Twin Eagles Picnic Ground.

A wooden foot bridge crosses Tarryall Creek and a well-defined path starts very gradually uphill through a dense growth of trees, interspersed with enormous boulders. At the top of the first hill the trail emerges into an open meadow where it splits. Go left at this point. Now the path enters a densely wooded area. If you choose to take this walk in summer the wild flowers are varied and profuse. If you are a person who enjoys Colorado's mountain flora you will find this to be a particularly rewarding hike.

The next trail junction is a well-marked one that directs you to Hankins Pass four miles to the east. This additional mileage is a possible side trip when you return, time and weather permitting. When you have walked about three miles the path bends around slightly and gradually ascends a rather rocky hill. Near the top the trail leads into a very muddy section. Just below the mud you pass through an area of large rock outcroppings, a very acceptable lunch stop.

From here you may wish to continue on to climb McCurdy Peak. If not, you could return to the trailhead, having walked six miles in all. It should be noted that all grades on this trail are gradual, with a scant 400 feet of elevation gain in the three miles you have already walked, making this an especially easy hike.

In autumn the profuse growth of aspen trees would rank this as a top area for color pictures. Therefore, the preferred seasons for the Brookside Trail would be summer and fall. Although we have not tried it in winter the well-protected, easy grades suggest that this could be an excellent snowshoe trail. While you will not be able to view the higher mountain ranges from the Brookside, it does offer scenic beauty of a more pastoral variety, as well as a relaxing stroll through a lovely wooded area.

The low altitude Brookside-McCurdy Trail traverses a grove of aspen trees at this point.

Here is another view along the Brookside-McCurdy Trail.

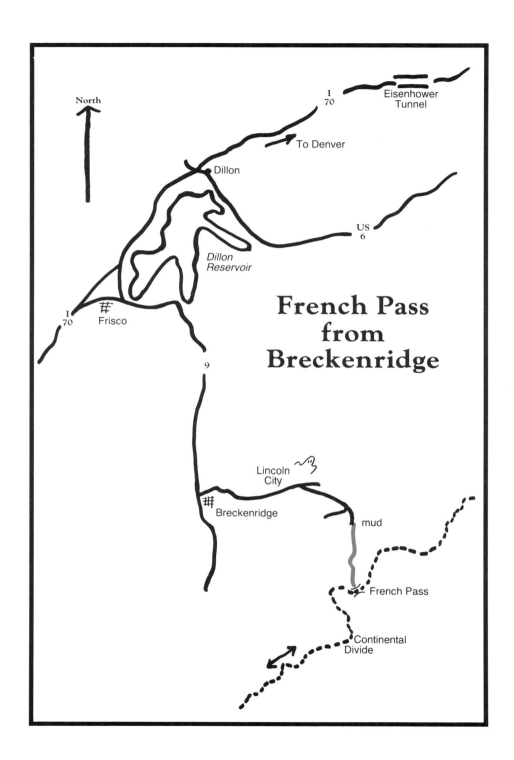

North

I
70

Eisenhower
Tunnel

To Denver

Dillon

US
6

*Dillon
Reservoir*

**French Pass
from
Breckenridge**

#
Frisco

I
70

9

Lincoln
City

#
Breckenridge

mud

French Pass

Continental
Divide

198

FRENCH PASS
from BRECKENRIDGE

This northwestern approach to French Pass, in common with the one from South Park, involves some rough road conditions on the way to the trailhead. However, the route on this side is not nearly as disagreeable as those encountered on the other side. Begin on Colorado Highway 9 which is also the main street through Breckenridge. Turn east at the lumber yard. If you stay on the main road it will take you up Lincoln Gulch, named for our sixteenth president. Because of extensive new home construction, several newer streets have been opened in the gulch. If in doubt, ask someone. At the head of the gulch the few remaining cabins of the ghost town of Lincoln City will be seen. In summer these structures are sometimes occupied by transients and their pets.

Just beyond the old town Lincoln Gulch becomes French Gulch. Stay on the main road and avoid side trails. Beyond the turnoff to Black Gulch the road bends abruptly south and deep mud holes attest the lack of maintenance. A car with 4-wheel drive helps here. Otherwise, probe the depth of the more suspicious looking puddles with a stick before driving through them. Depending on the season and the condition of the road, decide where you want to park, put on your pack and begin walking.

As you hike along the valley, the elevation gain is gradual. French Gulch is almost always green in season and a pretty little stream follows the path nearly to timberline. Colorful displays of native wild flowers bloom in the broad meadows. The dainty columbine, our state flower, is particularly abundant and the various hues of the Indian paintbrush can be vivid up here.

Going up from Breckenridge, the double ruts of the old French Pass
wagon road are clearly visible.

Evelyn Brown, Barbara Adams, and friend take time out on the
summit of French pass.

There is one point where an optical illusion may lead you off to the right, but the real trail is off to the left, beyond a large log. If you should lose the trail, walk to the left and find it again. At timberline the swale at the top of the pass can be seen, as well as the iron-tired wagon wheel scars that lead up to the summit. You are now within a mile or so of your destination. If the weather is good the view looking back down the valley is worth a picture. It improves as you continue walking. However, if the weather turns sour you should turn back immediately. Exposed, above timberline ridges on the Continental Divide are unsafe in an electrical storm.

From timberline to the top, the route is well-marked by the old scars. Except for a couple of steep pitches the elevation gain continues to be moderate. Depending on the place where you parked, the walking distance is about three miles each way. Accepting the same variable, the elevation gain is less than 2,000 feet for the three miles.

On our first visit to French Pass from the Breckenridge side, we left the town with Barbara and John Adams at 7:30 A.M. and were back down in plenty of time for a late lunch. We feel that much of the charm of French Pass rests with the fact that it has not been a particularly well-known trail. Even the American national flower, Kleenexus Americanus, does not bloom on French Pass.

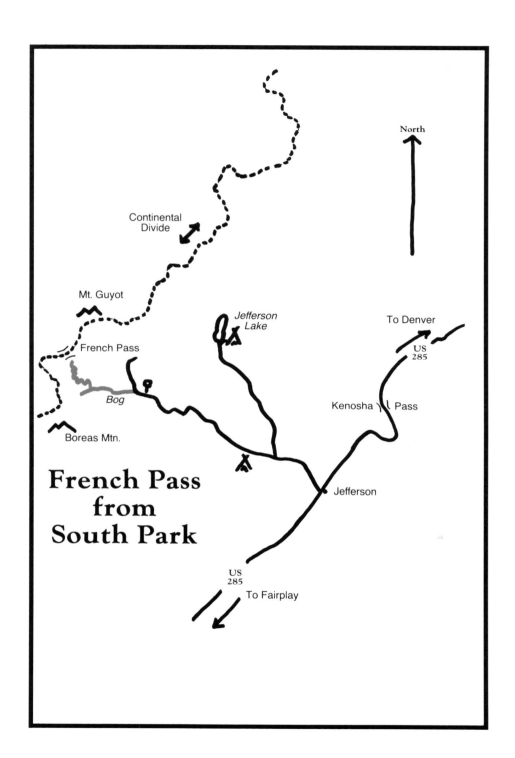

North

Continental
Divide

Mt. Guyot

*Jefferson
Lake*

To Denver

US
285

French Pass

Bog

Kenosha Y|(Pass

Boreas Mtn.

French Pass
from
South Park

Jefferson

US
285

To Fairplay

FRENCH PASS
from SOUTH PARK

For the sake of convenience many people tend to separate Colorado's nineteenth century years into two distinct epochs. First came the fur trade, then the mining period. Actually both movements overlap and in turn are overlapped by periods of exploration, the open range, and some other notable movements.

In the latter days of the fur frontier, many trappers were able to cash in on their knowledge of the mountains hiring out as guides to Colorado's "official explorers." Men like Kit Carson, Jim Bridger, and Thomas Fitzpatrick thus made the transition into a different lifestyle after the price of beaver pelts had plummeted downward.

Inevitably, since Frenchmen from Canada were among the personnel engaged in fur gathering, some of them also switched occupations. One such person was the man remembered in our history only as "French Pete." In common with other trappers, Pete found some of the crossings that became our earliest roads. Among them was a path that crossed the Continental Divide between South Park and the valley of the Blue River. Since these were two of his preferred trapping areas, a connecting trail was expedient. A gulch and a creek near present Breckenridge also bear the non-specific name of this pioneer.

In Colorado, the Continental Divide runs generally north and south with one notable exception. It curves abruptly around South Park where it runs east and west before assuming its conventional north and south direction once more. For this reason this initial approach to French Pass is mostly from the south, while the one detailed in the previous chapter comes from the north.

Because this is a rather obscure trail that appears only

on a limited number of today's maps, you should probably purchase a copy of the U.S. Geological Survey map of the Como quadrangle. Both approaches to French Pass are shown as dotted lines in the upper left hand quarter of the sheet.

Start your approach from US 285 at the town of Jefferson. Turn north on the graded county road toward Jefferson Lake. At the junction for the lake you should keep to the left and proceed toward the campground on the Michigan Creek road toward Georgia Pass.

Beyond the campground watch for a small sign that identifies French Creek. Turn left here onto an old trail that runs uphill and bends sharply to the right before entering an awesome bog, caused by seepage from the creek. Although this hole is loaded with old wood, rocks, and boards of later vintage, it seems to get worse by the year. We have seen people take a run at it in 4-wheel drive cars and sometimes they get through, but don't count on it. In dry years this hole dries out a bit in late September, but it remains rough. There is a short but equally bumpy by-pass that we cannot recommend. Negotiating either of these obstacles damages the environment, tries one's patience, and challenges the average vocabulary.

We suggest that you leave your car here as you are now just under six miles from the pass. Pick up the trail on the other side of the bog. For much of its distance you will be following a double rut wagon road, cut by later pioneers who followed French Pete's trail before better crossings were found. For most of the way the ruts follow the creek, occasionally crossing it as they gain altitude. Although the creek is never very far away, it is often beyond your line of vision as you proceed up the trail.

Stay with the main or most used trail. Further along there is a promising looking path to the left. Don't take it. It ends at an abandoned log cabin. Stay with the creek and keep to the right when in doubt. At one point the ruts drop steeply down to the creek and resume climbing with equal steepness beyond the creek. Here a ''No Vehicles Beyond This Point'' sign has been placed at the top of the grade.

From the South Park side, the trail to French Pass looks toward the
Continental Divide.

Near the top of French Pass, the trail becomes dim and crosses
a snow field.

The summit of the pass is now about two miles ahead. It continues as a double rut trail for the remaining distance to the top. One more steep pitch occurs shortly beyond timberline. Then the ruts turn black, suggesting possible low grade deposits of coal. Just short of the summit a broad field of hard snow blocks the path. Cutting or kicking step holes into the surface will help in getting across. Then you are on the top, 12,087 feet above sea level. Bald Mountain, 13,694 feet high, is the peak to your left or west, while 13,370 foot high Mount Guyot towers above you to the east.

Far below and to the north is the scar of the Wire Patch Mine, the broad valley that holds Breckenridge, and the peaks of the Tenmile Range. If you climb up that first ridge of Bald Mountain, you can enjoy a fine view of the trail you just traversed. South Park can be seen in the distance. Beyond it, the massive, dimly-outlined mountain is Pikes Peak.

In our opinion this is a single season hike. Try it only in late summer or in the autumn. Be sure to carry a camera. The views are memorable and the trail is rich in the history of a bygone era.

The foreground wagon ruts attest to the use of French Pass as a much-used route from South Park in the early days.

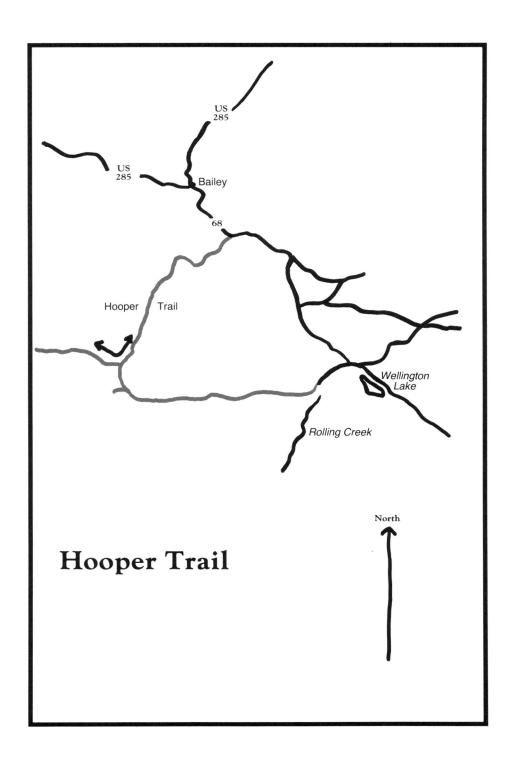

US 285

US 285

Bailey

68

Hooper Trail

Wellington Lake

Rolling Creek

North

Hooper Trail

HOOPER TRAIL

W.W. Hooper was a veteran of the Civil War, one of those who arrived in Colorado Territory in the rush of easterners following the conclusion of our fraternal struggle. Hooper's primary interest was timber. After homesteading an extensive trace near the present town of Bailey, he was determined to construct a lumbering road across the ridge to the south in order to cut and haul out logs from the Lost Park area. He completed work on the grade in the middle 1880s. But Hooper's trail saw very little use and government regulations stopped him. In later years he worked as a forest supervisor in the Leadville area. Today the Hooper Trail, somewhat over-grown here and there, is a pleasant low altitude hiking path in the Pike National Forest.

Access to the trailhead is provided by following Park County Road 68 southeast out of Bailey for eight miles. The first two miles are paved while the remaining six are graded. Watch for the marked Rolling Creek trailhead on your right. It is designated as #663 while the trail itself carries #1776. Leave your automobile in the small parking space and begin walking west on what appears to be a Forest Service access road. Continue for two and one half miles to the first trail junction. Here you will walk to the right for a half mile. At that point you intersect the Hooper Trail. Go to your left and hike along for another half mile to the creek. Here you should go to the right, following the creek for three and one half miles of pretty, rolling, wooded countryside.

The largest mountain in this region is 11,970 foot Windy Peak, clearly visible from the trail at this point. At the next intersection walk to your right along the primitive road for a short distance through private property. Do not trespass here, but continue on uphill to

Aspen trees line a section of the pretty Hooper Trail.

Larger trees shade the hiker along much of the Hooper Trail.

the road, Park County 68 again. Now go to the right and walk along the graded road for just over a mile back to the parking area where the hike began. Late spring, summer, or autumn are our preferred seasons for this historic walk through the forest.

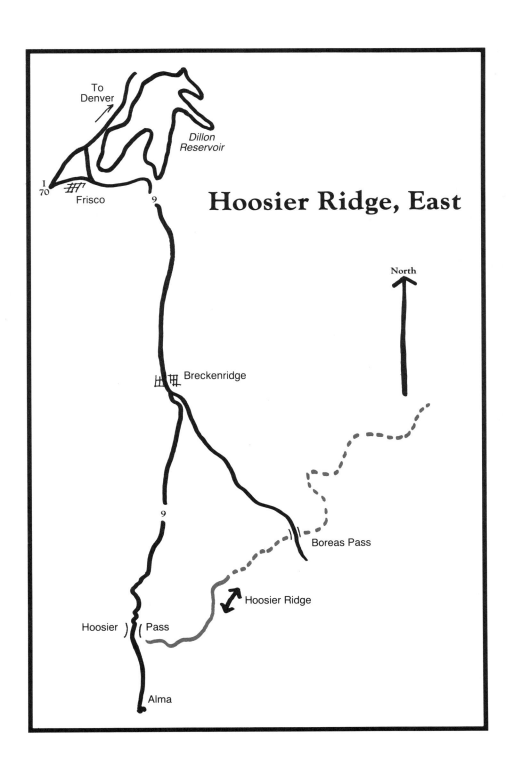

To
Denver

Dillon
Reservoir

I
70

Frisco

9

Hoosier Ridge, East

North

Breckenridge

9

Boreas Pass

Hoosier Ridge

Hoosier) (Pass

Alma

212

HOOSIER RIDGE, EAST

Whenever the terrain and the weather will permit it, walking the crest of the Continental Divide is an exciting and very scenic experience. Colorado's Hoosier Ridge is such a place. You can start from either Alma or Breckenridge and drive on Colorado State Highway 9 to the 11,543 foot summit of Hoosier Pass. This lofty crossing was named in the late 1870s by homesick miners from Indiana who were making their way to Leadville.

Park at the top of the pass in the large area near the sign on the west side of the highway. Now cross the road to the east, go around the metal gate and begin walking uphill along the service road that leads to the Mountain Bell relay building. At this point the road ends abruptly and there is no trail as such beyond this point. Merely start up the ridge by a route of your own choosing, moving east toward the highest point. We have enjoyed seeing water pippet nests on this slope, secreted beneath the clumps of tundra grasses.

Quite a colorful rotating display of seasonal wild flowers make this slope a lovely place in which to walk. In places the grades are quite steep, so stop to catch your breath now and then; everyone else does. At the ridge the altitude is 12,814 feet, making an elevation gain of 1,271 feet in less than two miles. Several rock cairns have been erected along the higher points of the ridge, in anticipation of the Continental Divide Trail that will one day be completed here and across Colorado.

Since this hike is some distance above timberline, observe the weather carefully and take appropriate precautions. We have encountered both snow and hail in profusion along this crest in July. Looking back toward the west, the massive rounded peak is Mount Bross. Next

At left, Mount Lincoln looms up above Montgomery Reservoir as viewed from an exposed ridge above Hoosier Pass.

Here are two of the rock cairns that mark the route along the Hoosier Ridge Trail.

to it and above the Montgomery Reservoir, the big mountain with a small domed summit is 14,286 Mount Lincoln, named by miners at Montgomery for our sixteenth President. Further to the right the big peak with the long ridge is 14,286 foot Mount Quandary, one of the easiest to climb among Colorado's higher peaks. The large body of water to the north is the Dillon Reservoir, a Denver water supply.

For a hike of a single day's duration we usually go as far along this ridge as the second summit. Here a semblance of a footpath leads up to the cairn-marked top. This is a scenic lunch stop when the weather is calm. If the wind is blowing, a condition not uncommon at this altitude, drop down into the next saddle for protection. Actually this ridge continues on and can be hiked all the way to Boreas Pass and beyond, a far more strenuous and quite demanding trek.

As described here, the distance to this point and the return to your car by the same route makes a round trip walk of about five miles. The best, and only, seasons for hiking along Hoosier Ridge are midsummer and early autumn. Be sure to bring sun glasses, adequate water, and a camera with color film.

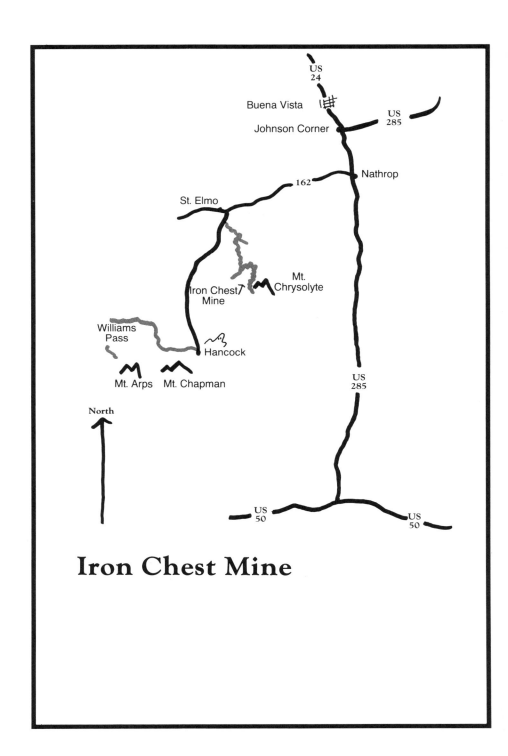

Iron Chest Mine

The IRON CHEST MINE

Although this hike is a moderately difficult one, it offers a combination of fine scenery and an interesting historical glimpse into the remains of a remote, century-old mining district. To reach the trailhead drive south from Buena Vista on US 285 to Nathrop. Turn west on Colorado Highway 162, which is now paved to a point just beyond the Mount Princeton Hot Springs. From the end of the pavement to the ghost town of Saint Elmo, you will be following a graded country road that was once a railroad grade. Instead of entering Saint Elmo, turn south or left at the edge of the old town and follow the old railroad line up the hill for five tenths of a mile toward the Romley and Hancock sites.

You will find parking for several cars at this point. The Iron Chest trail begins here, starting up to your left from the east side of the road. The route traverses the north western slope of 12,830 foot high Chrysolyte Mountain. The Iron Chest Mine lies about 1,000 feet below its summit. This is not a well-known trail and it is little used. No markers identify it. Be sure to wear sturdy shoes, carry a lunch and rain gear. When you have walked only a few yards the path divides. Keep to the right at this point. This is a somewhat steep, no nonsense trail. It begins climbing and it never lets up. It is also rocky and shows few signs of recent use. One can only feel pity for the mules that probably expired in harness while pulling loaded wagons on this grade.

When you reach the next junction go straight ahead. The less distinct trail branching to the left terminates at a mine. The same advice applies to the following junction, where another trail to the left also ends at a mine. Next comes an abrupt climbing switchback to the left. Avoid the less traveled path that leads straight ahead

At timberline, Evelyn Brown passes an abandoned ore loading chute
on the Iron Chest Mine Trail.

A few of the original buildings still stand at the old Iron Chest Mine.

from the point of the curve. Less than a quarter of a mile up, a second switchback will be found, turning the trail south again.

Just as you reach the last growth of aspen trees, a roofless cabin will be found on the right side of the trail. From this point on, watch for wild raspberry bushes. At this elevation they mature in mid-September and are a delicacy. Their profusion is evidence of how little traffic this trail has. We have seen deer at this point also. Now the trail becomes a long ledge as it climbs up through the last of the evergreen growth. There is one more junction, where the tree line occurs. Keep to the left here, but by this time the buildings of the Iron Chest Mine are in view above you, and it is obvious where the trail leads.

This final pitch is quite steep. An old boiler and an intact tram tower can be seen below the cluster of buildings. You are now at an elevation of 11,950 feet. The Iron Chest dates from 1879. Originally, the mine was entered through several short adits about fifty feet apart in elevation. The main shaft was approximately 400 feet below the crest of the ridge and to the south of the mine buildings. The main shaft was some 280 feet deep. From the principal shaft there are 2,000 feet of drifts that branch off on three levels. Some 400 feet of the lowest level was reached through the nearby Mary Murphy Mine on the southwest side of Chrysolyte Mountain.

The Iron Chest was on the northern extension of the Pat Vein of the Mary Murphy property. It is a filled fissure of the Mount Princeton monzonite. Its ore body ranges in width from one to six feet. In the beginning the ore was packed out on mules for refining at the mills in Pueblo. Later the tram line carried it down the mountain to Romley, almost directly below in the Chalk Creek Valley. Production from the Iron Chest continued well into the present century. Between 1905 and 1915 it produced 477 ounces of gold, 13,326 of silver, 1,535 pounds of copper, and 21,089 pounds of lead. The principal mineral was always quartz.

At this point you will have walked about four miles, gaining approximately 2,000 feet of elevation in the process. Working your way back down over the great numbers of large boulders that litter the old trail can be taxing on the knees, so take your time, picking your footing carefully. The best seasons for a trek to the Iron Chest would be mid-summer through early autumn. Total walking distance is eight miles.

A wooden tram tower can be seen from the interior of one of the abandoned structures at the Iron Chest Mine when looking west across the Chalk Creek Valley.

221

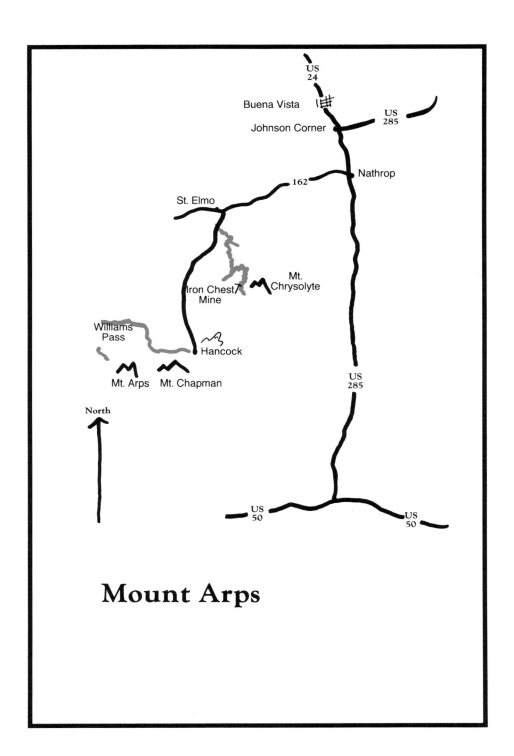

Mount Arps

MOUNT ARPS

This gentle 12,383 foot high mountain on the Continental Divide was named to honor the late Louisa Ward Arps, Dean of Colorado Historians. Its official designation, in 1988, is so recent that at this writing no maps show the peak by name. The 1940 USGS Garfield quad map shows it and the approach to it in good detail, but the 12,394 foot elevation is incorrect. Their 1982 Cumberland Pass map corrects the elevation but shows the route in less detail, and of course the new name is not shown there either.

Mount Arps is a very special place to us. Louisa and her husband, Elwyn, were our long-time friends, hiking and snowshoeing companions, and fellow history enthusiasts. They were our dinner guests on January 9, 1987, just two days prior to her death at age 84. Mrs. Arps had been a librarian at South High School, at the Denver Public Library, and at the Colorado State Historical Society. Both Elwyn and Louisa were active in our Colorado Mountain Club. Louisa authored many books, including our favorite, *Denver in Slices*. Elwyn died in 1990.

Louisa had a "pixyish" sense of humor. Once at a birthday dinner for my wife, she leaned across the table and smeared butter on Evelyn's nose. "That," she proclaimed, "is to help you slide into next year." Each New Year's eve at midnight Louisa always opened the back door to let the old year out, telling it what she had not liked. Next she would open the front door to admit the new year, enumerating what she expected of it. She was a dear and very special lady. Naming this mountain in the Sawatch Range for her and Elwyn was a much deserved honor.

To climb Mount Arps, follow the same directions as

Looking across the ghost town of Hancock, Mount Arps dominates
the western horizon.

Dr. Tom Noel and the author stand beside the rock cairn on the
summit of Mount Arps.

written in the Williams Pass chapter in this section. Briefly, drive to Buena Vista on US 285. Follow US 285 and US 24 south to Nathrop where you should turn west onto State Road 262. At the eastern edge of the ghost town of Saint Elmo turn left onto the dirt road to the ghost towns of Romley and Hancock. This poorly maintained grade was the route of the Denver, South Park and Pacific Railway. It is passable as far as Hancock. Park there and follow the abandoned grade around to the right or west, toward the Alpine Tunnel.

Walk about a half mile to the Williams Pass sign. Leave the railroad grade at this point and hike uphill to your left for two miles to the 11,262 foot high summit of the pass. At the top you will see two peaks to the east or to your left as you face south. The gradually rounded summit to the left is Mount Arps. The other summit, more pointed, is Mount Chapman.

Since no foot path exists on Mount Arps at this writing, choose your own route and climb up the remaining 621 feet of elevation to the above timberline top. If you work your way up to the south ridge, the grade is somewhat more gradual. Many species of wild flowers will be found all along the trail as well as on the peak itself. We saw columbine, bistort, and three colors of Indian paintbrush, among others. From the top you can look down on the site of Hancock. Above it and to the left, the large mine is the Mary Murphy. The grade that passes to the left of Mount Chapman is Hancock Pass. Far to the south, if the day is clear, Uncompahgre Peak is visible in the San Juan Range. Be sure to sign the register attached to the rock cairn on the summit. It was placed by Tom Ward, Louisa Arps' nephew.

From Hancock, the walking distance as described is three and a half miles each way. Be sure to carry a lunch, your camera, and sun glasses. From early July through mid-September are good times to enjoy Mount Arps.

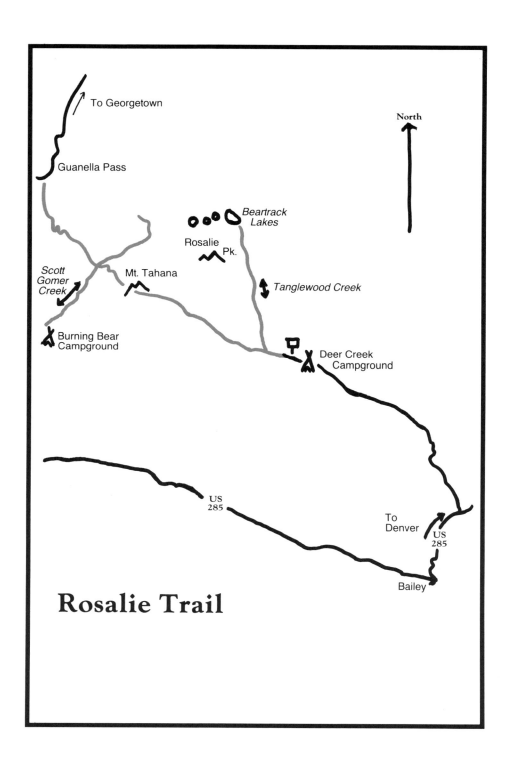

To Georgetown

North

Guanella Pass

Beartrack
Lakes

Rosalie
Pk.

Scott
Gomer
Creek

Mt. Tahana

Tanglewood Creek

Burning Bear
Campground

Deer Creek
Campground

US
285

To
Denver

US
285

Bailey

Rosalie Trail

ROSALIE TRAIL

For many years we had the pleasure of hiking with a couple who used to say, "There's a Rosalie Trail up there somewhere, but we have never found it." Well, the Forest Service has found it, and the trailhead is well marked at this writing. To reach it take US 285 from Denver up Platte Canyon. Turn off to the north (right) just before the top of Crow Hill. This is Deer Creek Junction and the road follows Deer Creek Valley. Stay on the main road beyond the end of the pavement, pass the Deer Creek campground and go on to the traffic circle where the road ends. Here is where the Rosalie Trail begins.

At the trailhead a new sign tells you that Guanella Pass is 12.5 miles ahead, a shelter house is found at 8.4 miles, and Rosalie Pass is 6.9 miles up the trail. Go through the gate displaying the "no vehicles" sign and keep to your left where the trails separate. The right branch goes up Tanglewood Creek and follows a rather wet path to Beartrack Lakes.

The Rosalie Trail follows the spine of the Deer Creek Valley, paralleling the creek for most of its length. Both deciduous and evergreen trees line the right-of-way and an abundant wild flower display can be enjoyed as you walk along. Although a lot of altitude is gained as you walk, the elevation rise is gradual. In all you will climb some 600 feet in the first six miles. From the clearings you will catch glimpses of Mount Tahana above you and to your right, but its summit is not yet visible from the deep valley.

By the time you have come up beside Tahana, a lot of altitude has been gained. Very soon now you will find yourself at timberline and the terrain begins to level out. Although there is no sign this is the point now identified by the Pike National Forest as Rosalie Pass. If you care to go on, there are a couple of interesting alternatives. Near this point a branch of the trail goes off to the left, running almost straight south, to Kataka and Spearhead mountains. It emerges by way of Threemile Creek at the Whiteside picnic ground in Geneva Gulch.

As a second choice you can continue on the main path up Deer Creek to the northwest. At the next junction a turn to the left (south) will put you on the Scott Gomer Creek Trail, which goes to the Burning Bear Camp Ground in Geneva Gulch. Some Pike National Forest personnel have called the high point on this ridge Rosalie Pass, although no current map credits the name at this writing. Rosalie Peak, 13,575 feet high, is visible to the east from this point. If followed to the end, the path climbs up out of Deer Creek to emerge on the summit of Guanella Pass, south of Georgetown.

If the automobile of a companion is parked at the Whiteside or Burning Bear campgrounds, these trails become less arduous as two car hikes. Merely drive back and pick up the original car that was left at the end of the Deer Creek road. The latest edition of the Pike National Forest map shows the entire group of routes of these trails, but it does not identify Rosalie Pass. Because of high altitude snow conditions, mid-summer through early autumn would be the preferred seasons for this hike.

From the Deer Creek side, the Rosalie Trail approaches the pass through a stand of evergreen trees.

From the top of Mt. Rosalie, well above the trail, we look across toward South Park.

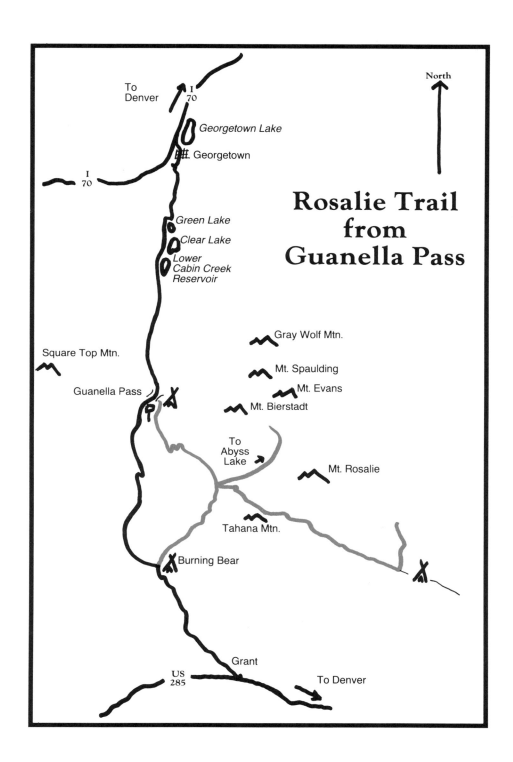

Rosalie Trail
from
Guanella Pass

To Denver

I 70

Georgetown Lake

Georgetown

I 70

Green Lake

Clear Lake

Lower Cabin Creek Reservoir

Gray Wolf Mtn.

Mt. Spaulding

Square Top Mtn.

Mt. Evans

Guanella Pass

Mt. Bierstadt

To Abyss Lake

Mt. Rosalie

Tahana Mtn.

Burning Bear

Grant

To Denver

US 285

North

ROSALIE TRAIL
from GUANELLA PASS

If the entire thirteen miles described in the previous chapter seems too long, the following approach from the summit of Guanella Pass presents an attractive alternative, and a more modest gain in elevation. The pass is an 11,669 foot high partly paved road that extends north and south, connecting Georgetown on Interstate 70 with Grant on US 285. The pass can be reached from either town. Guanella Pass lies just east of the Continental Divide but is not a major crossing. It is, however, one of Colorado's prettiest roads when the aspen trees have changed color in the autumn.

To follow this trail, park in the area provided on the summit of the pass. Begin walking south along the broad path from the parking lot adjacent to the metal Rosalie Trail sign. The Forest Service calls this path #603. It splits before you are out of sight of your car. Its right fork leads abruptly up over a hill. The easier, lower path swings around the east or left side of the same hill. Both routes converge again on the other side, so it is a matter of choice as to which trail one takes.

Although the course has now become narrower, it is double rutted at this point and is easier to follow across the treeless tundra. There are also rock cairns at intervals. When you have walked just over a half mile look off to your left. Barely above the jagged knife ridge of 14,060 foot high Mt. Bierstadt you will see the summit of 14,258 foot high Mt. Evans. From this angle its dormant crater is clearly visible. To the left or north of Mt. Bierstadt are Mt. Spalding and Gray Wolf mountain, both of which are in the 13,000 foot category. When you have walked another half mile turn and look to your right or west. The largest peak is Square Top Mountain.

The power lines north of its summit cross Argentine Pass, highest of all the North American crossings of the Continental Divide.

Now watch for a large rock cairn on the left side of the path. Beyond it take the narrower branch to the left and walk toward the cairn with a stick wedged vertically in its center. Follow the succession of cairns and sticks as you progress. The colored plastic ribbons on the cairn poles mark the trail for winter snowshoeing and for cross country ski enthusiasts. Here the trail traverses an extensive willow growth and the ground is soft and wet in some spots. As the path enters the stand of evergreen trees it loses elevation, dropping down to Scott Gomer Creek by a series of steep switchbacks. An arrangement of large rocks will help you to "boulder hop" across the creek, but a stout stick increases ones feeling of security.

On the opposite side the trail turns south again, gaining elevation as it traverses another willow growth. Once again rock cairns and pole markers are found at intervals. When you have reached the summit of the first ridge above the creek, take a look at the wooded hill on your right. There is a nice clearing on its crest with plenty of big boulders to sit on. You have now walked just over three miles and this is a fine lunch stop.

At this point you will need to decide whether to go on downhill, following the trail into the valley of Deer Creek. The other alternative is to retrace your steps back to the car, making this a total walk of six miles. Because of the altitude, the best times for this hike are from late June through early October. Although we have never done so, others have used this area for winter recreation.

At the top of Guanella Pass, a sign directs you to the Rosalie Trail.

The path in the foreground is the Rosalie Trail.

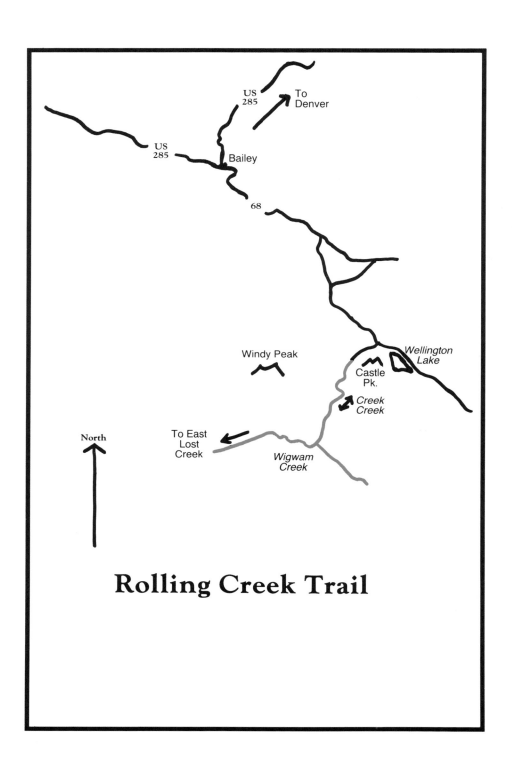

Rolling Creek Trail

ROLLING CREEK TRAIL

If you are a person who enjoys a varied display of Colorado wild flowers, try this hike in late June. Friends in Golden had told us about the pretty, wooded Rolling Creek Trail a couple of years prior to our first hike on it. To reach the trailhead take US 285 to Bailey. Leave the highway and turn left at the Standard station at the eastern edge of town. This is Park County Road 68. Follow this partly paved, partly graded road for 8.6 miles southwest into the Pike National Forest. The Rolling Creek Trail shares its trailhead with the Hooper Trail. After parking, walk about a half mile on the 4-wheel drive road. At that point a small marker directs that you turn left onto the Rolling Creek Trail.

As you enter the path a jagged peak appears off to your left. It is a mere 9,691 feet high and is called the Castle. The up and down grades encountered on this trail are easy ones. They gain and lose elevation gently. For much of the way the path parallels pretty little Rolling Creek. Crossings of the creek, where necessary, are accomplished on split logs.

In early summer you will find lots of wild flowers growing along both sides of the path. We have seen Colorado's state flower, the columbine, shooting stars, penstemon, and Indian paintbrush, among others. After you have walked a mile or so the trail enters an area of large boulders, becoming a bit steeper as it climbs up along a shelf above the creek. You will pass several busy little waterfalls before you enter a small wooded meadow.

The trees here are principally aspens and we like this spot as a cool and shady picnic stop. Beyond this point the trail becomes narrower and steeper. You have now gained 1200 feet of elevation in three miles of walking.

A crude but adequate bridge crosses Rolling Creek. The path can be
seen on the far side.

The jagged top of The Castle is at left while the Rolling Creek path
shows at the lower right.

236

If you choose to go on, the trail crosses the Kenosha Mountains at an elevation of 10,600 feet. Then it meanders down to a pack trail that parallels Wigwam Creek into East Lost Park. The alternative is to turn back at the meadow and return to the trailhead by the same route for a round trip walk of six miles. We prefer summer and autumn for the Rolling Creek Trail.

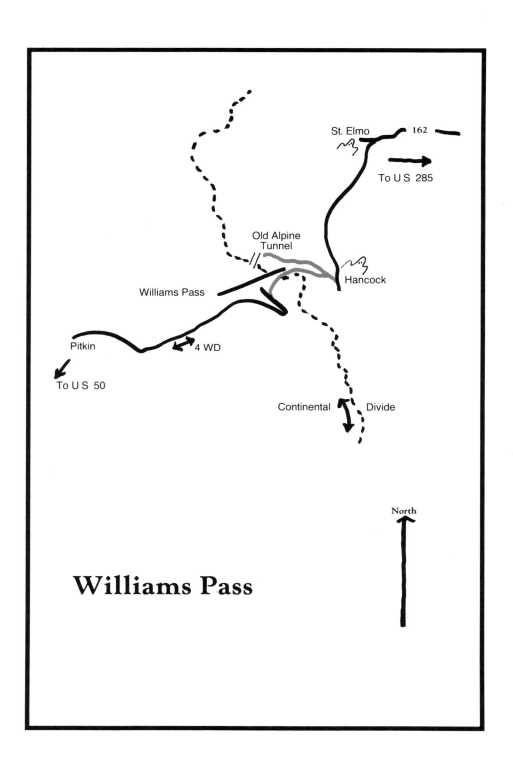

St. Elmo

162

To U S 285

Old Alpine
Tunnel

Hancock

Williams Pass

Pitkin

4 WD

To U S 50

Continental   Divide

North

Williams Pass

WILLIAMS PASS

Williams Pass was an early wagon and stagecoach road that was built to haul ore and supplies during Colorado's mining years. Although the Williams road made it possible to get across the Continental Divide, the terrain was and still is difficult. There are steep grades, big rock outcroppings, one huge boulder field, and at least three troublesome bogs of generous proportions. Eventually, better routes were found by which people might cross the range. When this happened, Williams Pass became a "has been."

During the 1950s and 60s this old trail was a formidable 4-wheel drive route, and local operators had many a lucrative field day extracting motorized tourists from the muck during summer months. Serious problems of erosion dictated a change to non-motorized status. Although no vehicular travel is currently permitted, enforcement is difficult. The restrictive signs are often destroyed, so you could have company on this trail. Nevertheless, Williams Pass is a fun place to hike as well as being historic.

To experience this walk, begin by driving to Buena Vista using US 285 and US 24. South of Buena Vista at Nathrop, turn west on State Road 162. Go on past Mount Princeton Hot Springs to the eastern edge of Saint Elmo, now a ghost town. Instead of entering Saint Elmo, turn left on the dirt road that runs uphill. Originally, this was the grade of the Denver, South Park and Pacific Railroad. It parallels Chalk Creek, passes the site of the abandoned town of Romley, and enters a third ghost town known as Hancock. About three trails lead out of Hancock. You should follow the abandoned railroad grade around the curve to the right. Do not attempt to drive beyond Hancock. Park here and begin walking. Since the other roads lack old ties and cinder pigmentation, the train route is easily identified. Walk northwest toward the Alpine Tunnel for just over a half mile. Watch for an old trail heading sharply uphill to the left. Avoid the first two left turns as they are merely opposite ends of a by-pass that goes around a wash-out on the trail.

This is the start of Williams Pass. The trail begins in a stand of evergreen timber, continues northwest for just over a mile, then turns southwest and crosses the range at an altitude of only 11,762 feet. If you walk north up the mountain on the right you will be rewarded with a rare view of both the eastern and western approaches to the Alpine Tunnel. Above the now blocked entrances to the Alpine Tunnel a thin trail is visible. It was called Altman Pass. At this point as well as when you reach the crest of Williams Pass, you are on the top of the Continental Divide. Here too is the boundary between the San Isabel and Gunnison National Forests, as well as the county line.

If you decide to continue on down the western side you will find a plainly marked trail. This side is somewhat rocky in places before it intersects the railroad grade once more. Actually, the Williams Pass road crosses the railroad grade just north of the great palisade and parallels it for some distance as it loses altitude entering the drainage of Middle Quartz Creek. From here down to the creek itself, the footing is much better on the railroad grade, but you may be sharing the trail with 4-wheel drive cars, legal on this side. The trail ends at Quartz Creek where a left turn will take you into Pitkin.

In the last century, Williams Pass was chartered under the name of the Alpine and South Park Toll Road. Before that, there was a usable path here dating back to Indian and fur trapping days. Two versions of the source of the Williams name still persist. One asserts that it was named for Rev. William S. "Old Bill" Williams, psychopathic trapper, cannibal and sometimes guide who made this crossing in the 1840s. The second story attributes its identity to Robert R. Williams, an assistance engineer for the Denver, South Park and Pacific Railroad.

240

On the way up from Tunnel Gulch, much of the Williams Pass Trail
shows evidence of wheeled vehicle travel.

Look west across the bog on the summit of old Williams Pass.

241

All things considered, this is a pleasant trail that is not overly well-known. It offers striking views of many lovely peaks and a couple of nice valleys. Summer and autumn would be the preferred seasons. If prior arrangements can be made, an automobile at each end of the trail eliminates the need for retraced steps. The distance from Hancock to Quartz Creek and the Pitkin road is roughly nine miles.

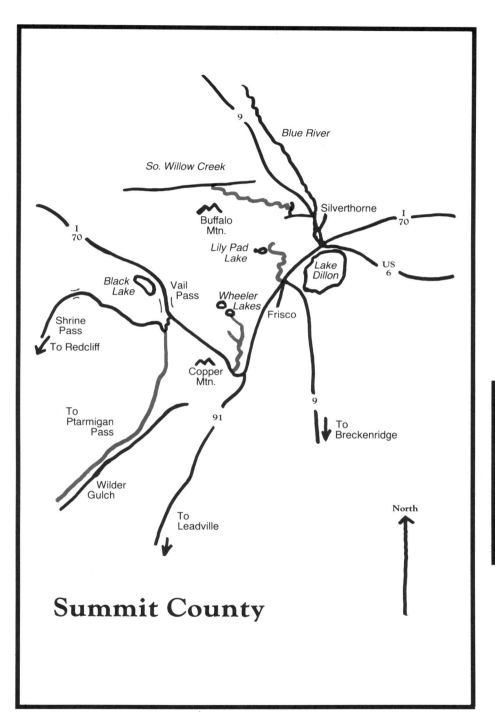

Summit County

Lily Pad Lake

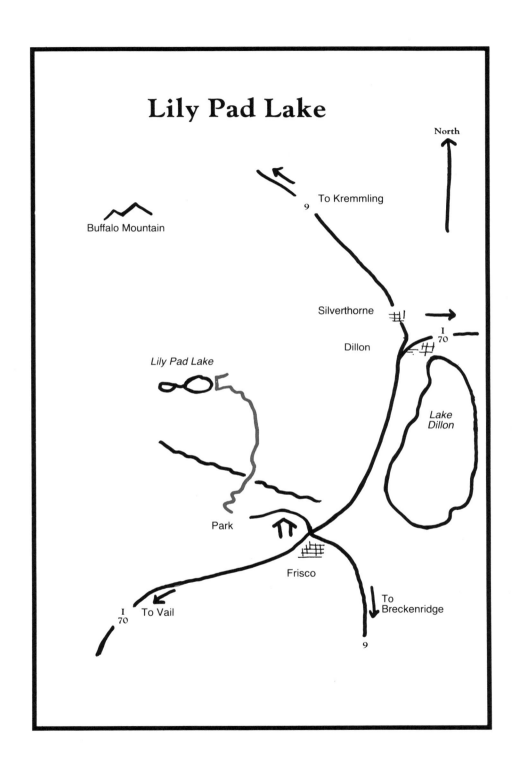

Buffalo Mountain

To Kremmling

9

North

Silverthorne

Dillon

I 70

Lily Pad Lake

Lake Dillon

Park

Frisco

To Breckenridge

I 70   To Vail

9

LILY PAD LAKE

During late September or early October, this short walk must surely be ranked among Colorado's loveliest hikes. The yellow aspen groves are profuse and colorful, the path is very distinct and the vistas of high snow-capped ramparts are both handsome and varied.

If you are driving west from Denver, follow Interstate 70 to Exit 38, which is marked for Frisco and Brecken-ridge. Leave the freeway by this ramp but do not turn onto State Highway 9. Instead, cross it and follow the graveled road that passes to the right or north of the wooden Information building. This road parallels Inter-state 70 for less than a quarter of a mile to the west and ends at a small parking area which functions as a trailhead for Lily Pad Lake. However, the sign at the start of the path says "Meadow Creek Trail."

For nearly its entire length, this is a tree-shaded, protected trail. It starts to climb rather steeply up from the parking area. In places two distinct ruts are visible, suggesting that this may have been a wagon road at one time. Elaborate barricades have been located strategically along the entire distance to the lake to keep motorized vehicles out. In several spots huge trees have been deliberately felled across the path. In other places the obstructions are more subtle. None of this, however, presents a problem for the pedestrian.

When you have walked less than a half mile, a crude log bridge provides a dry crossing of Meadow Creek. In places the trail levels off, traversing handsome groves of evergreen and deciduous trees, primarily aspens.

Mining ruins are visible at one point, but apparently it was not a very successful venture. Where the trail divides, go to the right. The left fork goes to the Gore Lake Trail and eventually on down to Vail. When you

From the trail to Lily Pad Lake, we look across Lake Dillon toward Grays and Torreys Peaks in the far distance.

Lily Pad Lake is at the end of the trail.

246

arrive at the next stream crossing, glance to the right for the crude arrangement of logs that will enable you to cross. On the other side the path turns sharply up to the left, passes an abandoned beaver colony and tops out on a ridge.

Stop at this overlook to enjoy a handsome view of Lake Dillon and the Continental Divide. Beyond the lake, the more prominent peaks are Grays and Torreys with Kelso beside them. Further to the right, two other mountains are seen: Mount Baldy and Boreas Peaks. Boreas and French Passes traverse those low saddles. Above the trail, the sharp, dominant peak is one of the summits of the Tenmile Range.

Now continue walking along the path as you are quite close to the lake. At Lily Pad you may choose to follow a path, crude in places, that circles the lake. From this path we have often seen ducks swimming along the shore line. Buffalo Peak, a landmark on the nearby Gore Trail, is the large mountain that looms up beyond the lake. The altitude here is 9,900 feet. The round trip hiking distance is a pleasant four miles, perhaps a bit less.

This is a fine hike for summer or in late spring if the snowfall has been a bit scanty, but the steeper parts would make it undesirable as a snowshoe trail. As already indicated, our favorite season for this walk is autumn.

Ptarmigan Pass

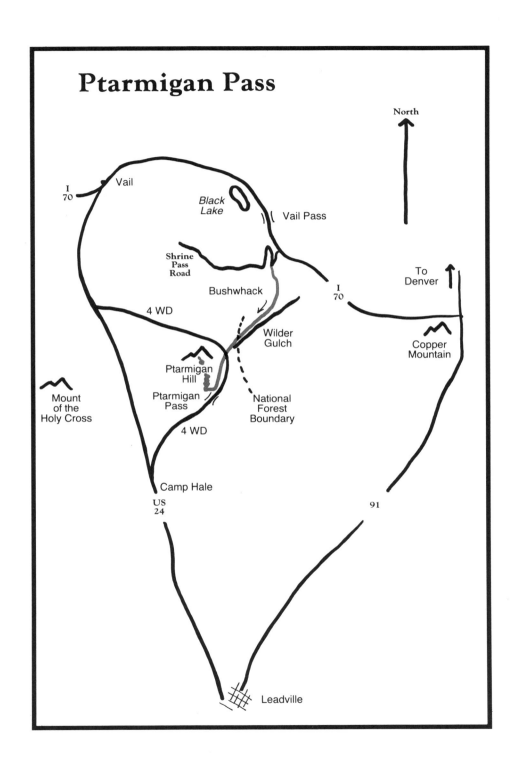

North

Vail

I 70

Black Lake

Vail Pass

Shrine Pass Road

Bushwhack

I 70

To Denver

4 WD

Wilder Gulch

Copper Mountain

Ptarmigan Hill

Mount of the Holy Cross

Ptarmigan Pass

National Forest Boundary

4 WD

Camp Hale

US 24

91

Leadville

PTARMIGAN PASS

Colorado has three Ptarmigan Passes, a Ptarmigan Peak, and a Ptarmigan Mountain. Two of the passes are in the Breckenridge-Vail area while the other is in the San Juans. The one that is the subject of this chapter has long been accessible by 4-wheel drive vehicles, but only recently by a hiking trail. The route described here is the one preferred by the Colorado Mountain Club. To reach the trailhead you should drive northwest on Interstate 70 from the Copper Mountain-Wheeler Junction intersection. Leave the freeway at the Shrine Pass exit and cross over to the west side. Your car can be parked in either of the two designated and quite visible parking areas.

Now comes the tricky part. Walk directly southwest from the parking area, cross the creek, and bushwhack across the ridge into Wilder Gulch. No trail crosses the ridge at this writing. Merely pick the path of least resistance through the willows and dead trees. From the ridge crest while walking downhill toward the little stream, you will presently encounter an old and overgrown double rut wagon road. Turn right on this road. It parallels the stream and follows Wilder Gulch.

As you look southwest up the gulch, 11,800 foot high Ptarmigan Pass is in the saddle between the two highest peaks. This is the view that is shown in one of the accompanying photographs. Ptarmigan Peak, with a small structure on its summit, is the mountain to the right of the pass. The path you are following stays well above the creek for the entire distance, but you must cross one or two of its little tributaries on stepping stones as you continue on up the hill. When you have walked about a mile and a half there are two huge trees that have fallen across the path. Just beyond this point is the White

The low saddle in the distance is Ptarmigan Pass. The trail follows the open valley.

From the ridge above Ptarmigan Pass, both Notch Mountain and Mount of the Holy Cross are clearly visible.

River National Forest boundary. Shortly after crossing the boundary the trail intersects a 4-wheel drive road that comes up from the Camp Hale site on Colorado State Highway 91. Turn left on this road and follow it to the pass. Some of the pitches are fairly steep and most of the grades are above timberline. Motorized company is possible here.

From the top both the Gore and Sawatch Ranges are clearly visible. Mount Elbert and Mount Massive, Colorado's two highest mountains, are the most prominent mountains to your left. Behind you the rugged Gore Range pierces the sky with many jagged summits. The best view of all is obscured by 12,130 foot high Ptarmigan Hill. Climbing it will add another steep mile but the view is worth it. There are two buildings on the top instead of one. After catching your breath, look to the west for one of the finest views of the Mount of the Holy Cross. This is a great lunch stop and a fine place from which to take pictures. A telephoto lens is a good idea, if available.

Your return is by the same route, making the total distance you have walked just under six miles. Because of the exposed nature of most of this terrain, late summer and autumn would be the preferred seasons.

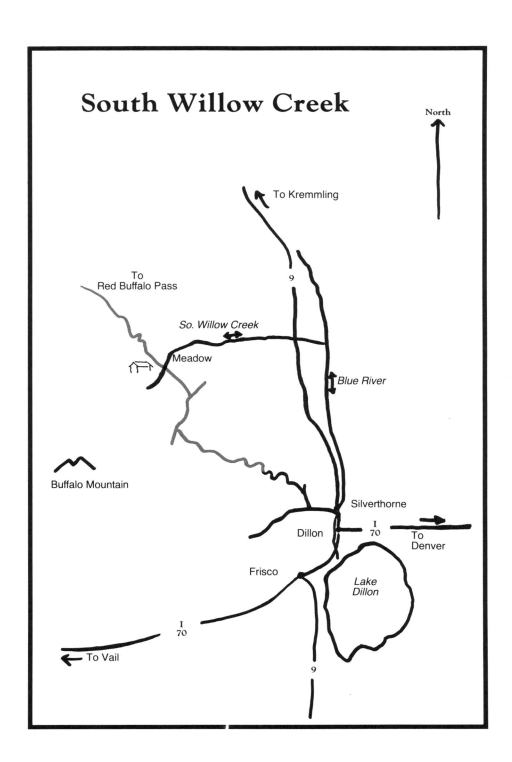

South Willow Creek

North

To Kremmling

To
Red Buffalo Pass

9

So. Willow Creek

Meadow

Blue River

Buffalo Mountain

Silverthorne

Dillon

I
70

To
Denver

Frisco

*Lake
Dillon*

I
70

To Vail

9

SOUTH WILLOW CREEK

This is an especially beautiful Western Slope hike that begins on a hillside above the town of Silverthorne and the Dillon Reservoir. From the Eastern Slope, follow Interstate 70 west through the Eisenhower Tunnel. Leave the freeway at the Silverthorne exit and drive west, crossing the Blue River. Turn left onto the first road after you have crossed the bridge. Drive about 400 feet on this graded road and turn right. A series of switchbacks will carry you up onto the ridge to the trailhead. This somewhat confusing maze of roads will probably become more complicated as new ones are cut to accommodate the mushrooming growth of new condominiums.

If in doubt you can always inquire locally for instructions to the South Willow Creek trailhead on the Gore Trail. At this writing, the trailhead is marked and limited parking is available for a few cars across the road from the sign.

Leaving the trailhead, you will walk northeast on the main Gore Range Trail. This is a pleasant trail, mostly shrouded in a dense growth of trees at this point. After gaining a limited amount of altitude, you will arrive at a place where the path splits. Take the left fork and walk toward Red Buffalo Pass. This branch of the trail leads mostly west and slightly south in a few places. It continues along through wooded country until it levels out as you enter a large open meadow. The prominent peak to your left is 12,777 foot Buffalo Mountain. Toward the western edge of the meadow the path skirts around an old log cabin, one of the few man-made landmarks along this route.

Beyond this point the trail climbs sharply up around a series of rocky cliffs. Where it passes a large rounded rock outcrop on the left is a good place to pause for a

The South Willow Creek Trail passes through a lush meadow on the way to Red Buffalo Pass.

Near timberline, the South Willow Creek Trail crosses a rocky ledge.

nice view back toward the east. Grays and Torreys Peaks are visible on the distant horizon. We think this spot makes a pretty fair lunch stop as you have now walked about five miles. If you continue on up to Red Buffalo Pass before returning to the trailhead, you will have walked more than twelve miles.

Although long, this hike is pleasant, mostly in shade and offers a variety of scenery. The best panorama is from the top of the ridge. We prefer summer or early autumn as the most appropriate seasons for this hike.

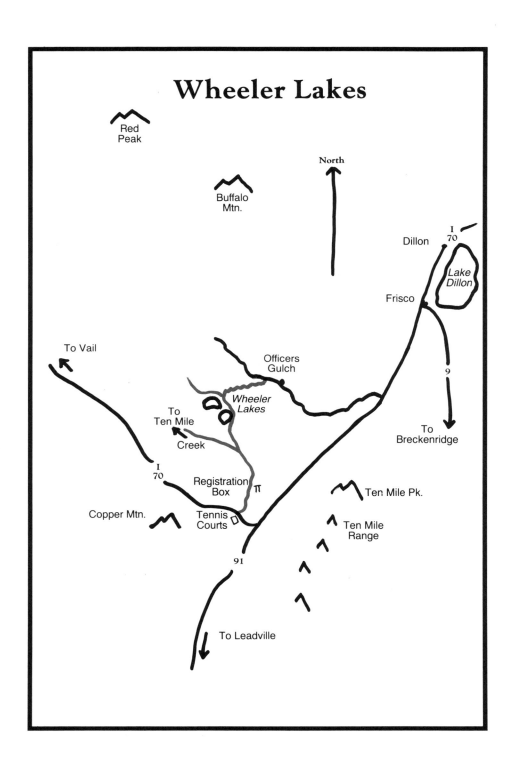

Wheeler Lakes

Red Peak

Buffalo Mtn.

North

Dillon

I 70

Lake Dillon

Frisco

To Vail

Officers Gulch

Wheeler Lakes

9

To Breckenridge

To Ten Mile

Creek

I 70

Registration Box

Ten Mile Pk.

Copper Mtn.

Tennis Courts

Ten Mile Range

91

To Leadville

WHEELER LAKES

The Wheeler Lakes trail starts from a point barely west of the junction of Interstate 70 and Colorado Highway 91. This large, open meadow has long been known as Wheeler Flats. All of the various Wheeler names in this area honor John S. Wheeler who came to Colorado in the gold rush of 1859. He moved to present Summit County in 1879 and established a hay ranch on Wheeler Flats. Soon a small community called Wheeler Junction grew up around the ranch. By 1880 Wheeler had wangled a post office for his town. Today the Wheeler Cattle Trail, one peak, the lakes described in this chapter, and a few other things still bear his name.

The trailhead for Wheeler Lakes lies directly north across Interstate 70 from the Copper Mountain tennis courts. At this writing it is marked by a stained wooden post implanted just above the frontage road. Actually this is the southern beginning of the Gore Trail, but you will walk only the first three miles to the lakes. Where the trail begins the altitude is 9,800 feet. You will gain 1,200 feet in the distance up to the lakes. Historically, this path seems to have been an extension of the old Wheeler stock trail from South Park. On that side it crosses the eastern escarpment of Quandary Peak before climbing up through the Ten Mile Range by a low saddle between Peaks 8 and 9.

As you climb steadily up the hill from the trailhead, a series of rock cairns and blazed tree trunks mark the path. A Forest Service registration box is nailed to a tree at the end of the first mile. You should sign your name here. Looking back behind you the large peaks on the horizon to the south are called Pacific, Crystal, Fletcher, and Wheeler. At a distance of two and a half miles the trail divides, with one branch going off to the North

Fork of Ten Mile Creek. Keep to the right here and continue on toward the lakes. There are two Wheeler Lakes, barely separated by the extruding shoulder of a wooded hill. The lakes drain downhill to the northeast into Officers Gulch.

Upon reaching the second lake, walk around it and go up to the ridge behind it. From this vantage point, both the approach to the Eisenhower Tunnel and Lake Dillon may be seen off to the northeast. To the north the trail to Uneva Pass is seen climbing up the ridge. Beyond the pass the trail goes up to Lost Lake and Red Buffalo Pass with connections to the North Willow Creek Trail and Boulder Lake.

Summer and autumn are the preferred times for this trail. If you care to make a backpack trip of several days, the Gore Trail extensions of this trail to the north offer endless possibilities. Be sure to secure good maps and a compass if you choose this latter alternative.

The scenic trail to Wheeler Lakes has beautiful panoramas.

The larger of the Wheeler Lakes is a pleasant lunch stop.

This young elk, with antlers in velvet, is typical of the large numbers of these graceful animals to be found throughout Colorado's high country.

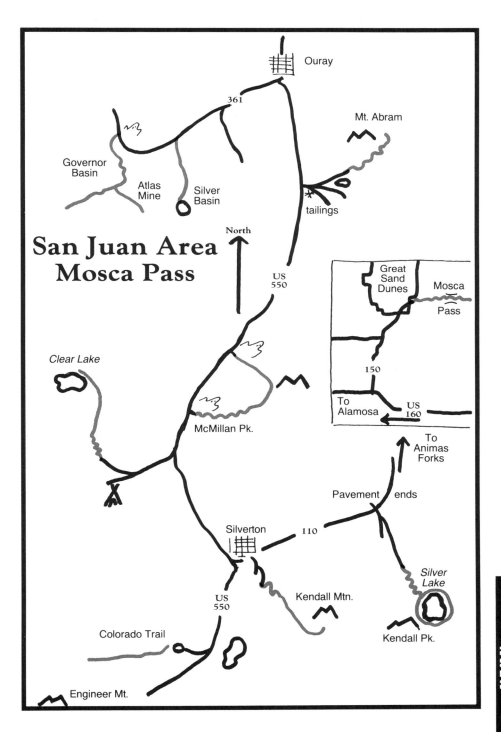

San Juan Area Mosca Pass

Ouray

361

Mt. Abram

Governor Basin

Atlas Mine

Silver Basin

tailings

North

US 550

Great Sand Dunes

Mosca Pass

150

To Alamosa

US 160

Clear Lake

McMillan Pk.

To Animas Forks

Pavement ends

Silverton

110

Silver Lake

US 550

Kendall Mtn.

Kendall Pk.

Colorado Trail

Engineer Mt.

San Juan
AREA

261

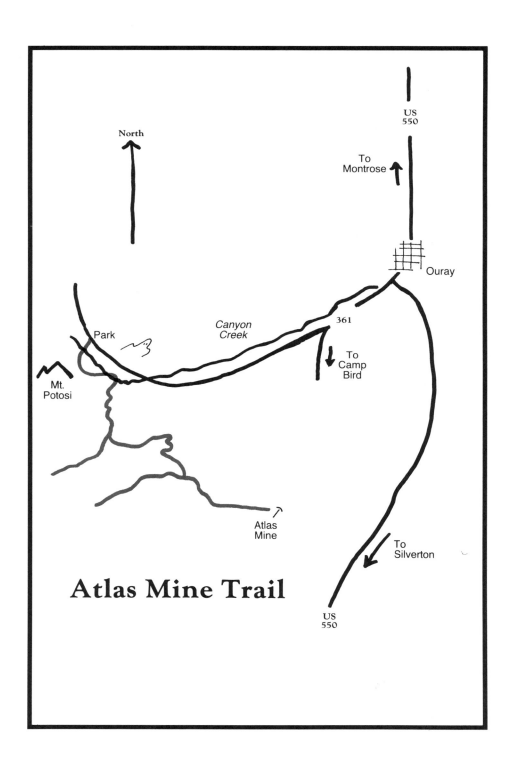

North

US
550

To
Montrose

Ouray

Park

Canyon
Creek

361

To
Camp
Bird

Mt.
Potosi

Atlas
Mine

To
Silverton

Atlas Mine Trail

US
550

ATLAS MINE TRAIL

The Atlas Mine Trail is short, steep, and begins at a trailhead that is somewhat difficult to reach. Start by taking County Road 361 southwest up Canyon Creek from Ouray. Take the right fork from Camp Bird and continue on up past the ghost town of Sneffels. Go beyond Sneffels for one mile, go left there and cross the creek by the first junction. If you have not already chosen to do so, leave your car at this point and begin walking. There have been years when this so-called road is both impassable and impossible to drive much beyond the junction to Camp Bird, unless you happen to have a 4-wheel drive vehicle.

As you cross Canyon Creek from the trail above Sneffels, look up to your right and enjoy the magnificent little waterfalls with the high peaks around Mount Potosi looming in the background. This is the area where the Coors brewery television commercials are filmed, showing a full glass of their brew on a rock beside the fast moving cascades.

Above this point the road becomes both steep and narrow. As it bends left you will again cross Canyon Creek. Look uphill along the creek from this point. The very crooked spires along the high crest is called St. Sophias Ridge. Telluride lies beyond it and almost straight down. In case you are interested, there is a rugged foot trail that crosses over from high in Governor Basin. It zig-zags down the other side into Telluride. Incidentally, this trail that you are now on goes up into Governor Basin to another trailhead described in this book.

Beyond the creek, the trail continues to bend to the left as it climbs steeply along the shelf of a sheer rock wall. Next it rounds a corner to the right and the view is

263

superb. Now start watching for a sharp switchback to the right from which a dim trail heads downhill to the south from the point of the switch. This is the Atlas Mine Trail, and from this point down to the mine the distance really is short. The path runs for about three quarters of a mile to the ruins of the huge old mine, losing some elevation in the process. A second trail leaves this same curve and heads steeply up into Sidney Basin.

The Atlas Trail, although narrow, is shrouded in a growth of trees and deciduous shrubbery. For photographic purposes there are several places from which you can frame mountain panoramas between tree branches for handsome compositions. At the Atlas location, a great quantity of equipment is still lying about. Directly below the mine was the huge Atlas Mill in the town of Sneffels. Its foundations are best viewed when you pass the town again on the way down. An overhead cable tramway carried the ores down from the mine to the mill for refinement.

Because of the altitude and the steepness of the surrounding slopes, this brief mile and a half walk is best hiked in summer and autumn.

The Atlas Mine trail holds lots of abandoned debris, including badly bent old mine railroad rails.

Evelyn Brown stands between the rails in a cut on the trail leading to the Atlas Mine.

Clear Lake

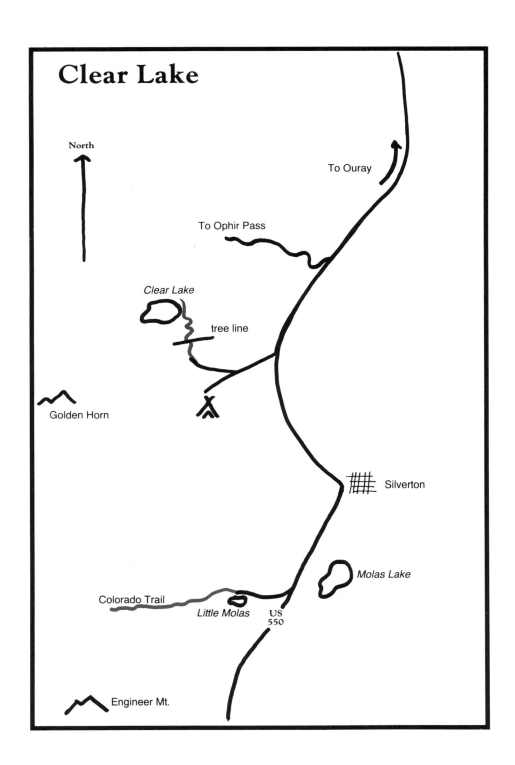

North

To Ouray

To Ophir Pass

Clear Lake

tree line

Golden Horn

Silverton

Molas Lake

Colorado Trail

Little Molas

US
550

Engineer Mt.

266

CLEAR LAKE

In our opinion, Colorado's San Juan Mountains include the most spectacular scenery in the state. Although the trails are somewhat narrower and usually steeper than most others in the state, the vistas are worth the effort. Over the years we have taken dozens of the hikes in this "Switzerland of America" and have yet to be disappointed. Clear Lake is merely one more such place. Its altitude is barely shy of 12,000 feet, well above timberline. The lake itself lies at the bottom of a steep-sided glacial cirque with huge barren peaks rising over a thousand additional feet all around it. Recently a little mining has been done above the south side of the lake, resulting in improvements to the trail in order to accommodate 4-wheel drive cars and trucks. It is still not a great road and we always prefer to walk for at least the last couple of miles to the lake. This preference depends on the season and the condition of the grade.

A short drive on US 550 north of Silverton will take you to a graded road that leads to the South Mineral Creek campground. Turn west onto this road and follow it to the junction a short distance before the campground. Turn right or west onto this road and drive as far as conditions and your judgement permits. There are several pretty nice vantage points along this route that afford good clear picture angles for a very jagged 13,894 foot high mountain called the Golden Horn. The road becomes steep before you are out of the trees and continues to angle up sharply beyond the tree line.

There is a good spot to leave your car about two miles below the lake. Here is a sharp switchback and a deep field of snow that usually persists well past mid-July. We usually walk from here. In summer the wild flowers are profuse both above and below the trail, including great

San Juan
AREA

Looking east across the San Juans on the Clear Lake Trail, we see hikers near the end of the path.

Clear Lake lies at the base of its above timberline cirque.

268

clusters of columbine, Indian paintbrush, bistort, and many others. At the lake we always seem to walk around to the right and picnic on the tundra. We have been told that fishing is good up here but we have never actually seen anyone catch anything.

The return to your car follows the same route. As described, you will have walked in the neighborhood of four miles, round trip. Barring an early snow, we prefer mid-summer or early autumn for this trek. Be sure to carry a camera.

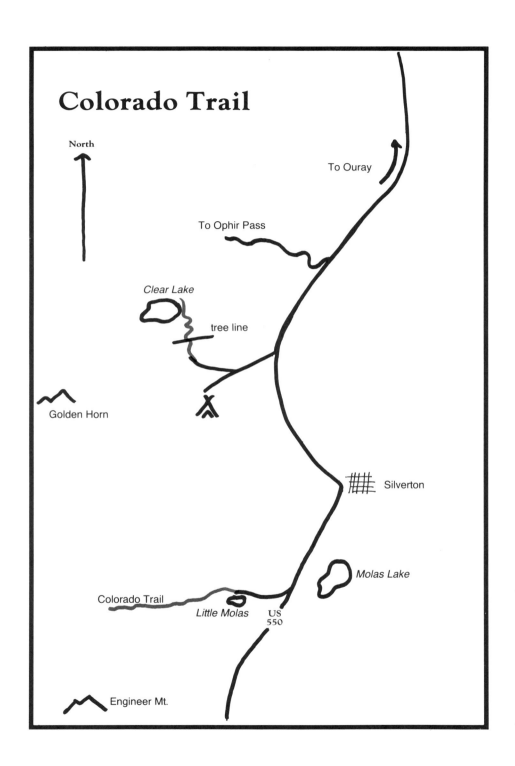

Colorado Trail

North

To Ouray

To Ophir Pass

Clear Lake

tree line

Golden Horn

Silverton

Molas Lake

Colorado Trail

Little Molas

US
550

Engineer Mt.

The COLORADO TRAIL

On October 2, 1968, Congress passed the National Trails Systems Act, a piece of legislation designed to provide access to wilderness pathways. By so doing, our Congressmen recognized that padding about the countryside on Vibram lug soles is a pastime worth preserving. The immensely popular Appalachian Trail, the Pacific Crest Scenic Trail, the Continental Divide Trail, and some others already exist.

Our Colorado Trail is the most recent addition to this group. It begins near Strontia Springs in Waterton Canyon near Denver. It ends either 450 or 485 miles away, depending on your source, at Durango. With assistance from the U.S. Forest Service and the Colorado Mountain Club, construction by volunteers began in 1972. Mrs. Gudy Gaskill has been the grand matriarch and principal driving force behind the effort. Gudy is a six-foot tall grandmother, loved and admired by all of us who have been privileged to know her. Without her, this lovely path probably would not exist.

The volunteers who have labored under Gudy's tutelage pay twenty five dollars each for the privilege of working as a trail builder for a week or more at a time. They have included former Governor and Mrs. Richard Lamm and astronaut Scott Carpenter. Food was provided without cost. Completion of the trail occurred in September of 1987, with formal dedication in July of 1988.

This is a family trail. In no instance do the grades ever exceed seven to ten per cent. Hiking time for the entire trail has been estimated as requiring six to seven weeks. Towns like Denver, Leadville, Breckenridge, and Silverton are close enough to the route so that supplies may be purchased along the way. If you are interested, a book titled *Guide to the Colorado Trail* describes the actual route as well as the historical and geologic features along the way. There are dozens of access points where one may walk for a day or more to sample the scenic beauty of the Colorado Trail.

We have chosen Little Molas Lake as our trailhead for this chapter. It will put you on one of the last to be completed sections of the trail. To find it, drive south of Silverton on US 550. Go past Molas Lake, a lovely spot where MGM filmed *Across the Wide Missouri* with the late Clark Gable. A short distance beyond the lake a graded road leaves the pavement by a sign designating Little Molas Lake. Turn right or west beside this sign. Follow the grade uphill to the lake, park and locate the distinctive trail markers. The grades are easy as the path runs generally southwest. You will gain some elevation, but only very gradually. The prominent peak on the horizon to the southwest is Engineer Mountain. It is one of two peaks in southwestern Colorado that share the same name.

Small white triangles affixed to posts or trees mark the way. While hiking on this section we met a pack train composed of seven llamas and two packers from Durango. This outfit regularly transported food and needed supplies to the trail crews who were working some miles further up the trail. In all we walked about six miles through some of the area's finest scenery. Obviously, the distance you travel will be determined by the weather and the stamina of the people in your party.

In future summers we intend to hike on many other portions of this spectacular Colorado Trail and we heartily recommend it to you.

A view looking southeast toward Little Molas Lake shows the well-graded Colorado Trail.

On the Colorado Trail, llamas transport food and supplies to the trail crews. Evelyn Brown is at the left of the path.

Governor Basin Trail

GOVERNOR BASIN

Despite the fact that walkers may find themselves sharing the trail with 4-wheel drive vehicles, this beautiful area remains a favorite hiking place for Colorado Mountain Club members who hold frequent outings in nearby Yankee Boy Basin. Governor Basin is a gem of nature, a lovely above timberline meadow surrounded by lofty snow-crested peaks. It is carpeted during most of the summer with fragile and colorful wild flowers. Tiny icy streams, unpolluted by civilization, come chuckling down from the great mountain barrier.

To see Governor Basin, drive five miles up the Canyon Creek road from Ouray. At the Camp Bird Mine junction, turn right for two bumpy miles to the ghost town of Sneffels. Very carefully now, drive one additional mile to the next junction. Better yet, park at Sneffels and walk to the junction. A 4-wheel drive car will enable you to continue beyond the junction, but the road really is much rougher from here on and becomes much steeper. Go left at the junction, pausing to view the twin falls to the right of the trail. These are the waterfalls shown in all those Coors commercials.

At first the trail runs southwest, then it turns toward the east, making a series of climbing switchback turns. At the point of one switchback, a trail to the left leads to the Atlas Mine. Finally the main trail bends to the southwest again, entering Governor Basin at an altitude of 11,600 feet. High above, at an altitude of 12,200 feet, the once great Virginius Mine clings to the sheer basin wall. North of the Virginius and across the basin are the remains of the Mountain Top Mine building.

If you care to pursue it further, the trail turns to the south and climbs up to the 12,600 foot level. It ends precipitously at the Humboldt Mine barely below Saint

Sophias Ridge. From this point the view is spectacular with 12,698 foot Stony Mountain to the north and 13,275 foot Mendota Peak to the south.

To the east of Mendota a steep and narrow pass crosses over Saint Sophias Ridge at 13,337 feet into Marshall Basin. From there it can be followed down into Telluride. Predicting an optimistic season for enjoying Governor Basin is difficult. Heavy snows come early, remain late at this elevation and some years are worse than others. Generally mid-July through early September should be safe, but don't count on it. It could snow at any time. To be safer, inquire in Ouray before starting up. Be sure to carry a camera and plenty of color film.

The abandoned structures of the Mountain Top Mine are in the Governor Basin.

From the trail up to Governor Basin, hikers get a view of square-topped Potosi peak.

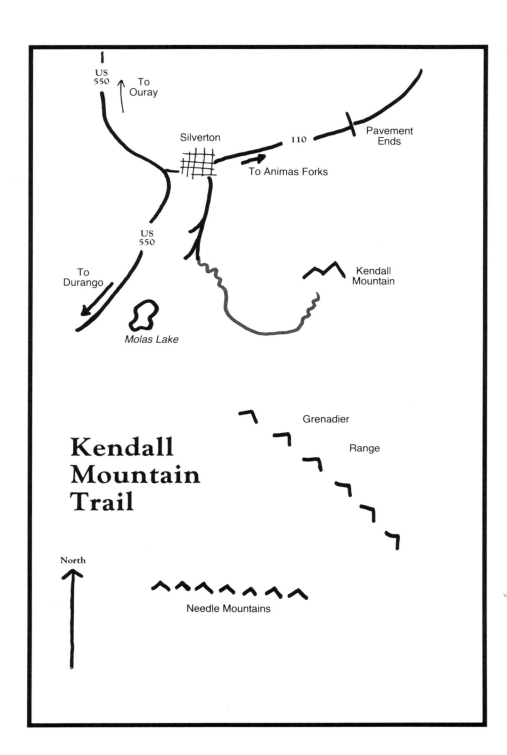

US
550

To
Ouray

Silverton

Pavement
Ends

110

To Animas Forks

US
550

To
Durango

Kendall
Mountain

Molas Lake

Grenadier

Range

Kendall
Mountain
Trail

North

Needle Mountains

KENDALL MOUNTAIN

Kendall Mountain offers just about any sort of a hike that you may care to make out of it. We have seen many back packers begin at Silverton, elevation 9,305, and walk all the way up to Kendall's 13,066 foot summit. The old Deer Park Trail is now a passable 4-wheel drive trail that reaches nearly to the top, leaving a walk of only a mile.

The Deer Park Trail begins on Silverton's southeast side, runs south, then turns east around Kendall's south slope. There are only two major junctions. Keep to the left in each instance. The first skirts around Kendall and may go back up onto the ridge behind Silver Lake. The second road goes off to the right, actually straight ahead, to an above timberline copper mine. Turn sharply left at this junction and continue up the switchbacks. When you reach the point from which Silverton becomes visible in the valley far below you, stop for lunch, and take some pictures.

From this vantage point you may look south down the Animas Canyon. At noon the train from Durango pulls into town. Viewed from up here, the perspective is certainly different. Just to the right of the Animas Canyon, US 550 can be seen winding its way south past Molas Lake, Molas Divide, Engineer Mountain and beyond. US 550 also runs northwest, then north around Anvil Mountain on its way to Ouray. The Red Mountains near Ironton Park can be seen, also the Silverton Red Mountains. Next comes Cement Creek, straight north out of Silverton. To the right, the Animas Valley is mostly obscured by the mass of Kendall Mountain.

Now follow the rocky trail up to Kendall's summit for an improved extension of the panoramic view. There are two wooden markers on the top. The view from either is sensational. Far to the south the Needle Mountains are now in full view. To the northeast, the Animas Valley winds its way up toward Cinnamon Pass. From this point Kendall Peak lies almost due east, rising high above the cirque that holds Silver Lake. Truly, this is a place where one can stand believing that you are the only person in the world, and that the handsome vista spread out before you would stay as it was, forever.

The panorama from the top of Kendall Mountain shows Red Mountain Pass, at left, and Cement Creek at the right. The town is Silverton.

Evelyn Brown is on the Kendall Mountain Trail. Arrow Peak is above here in the distance while US 550 appears at the right.

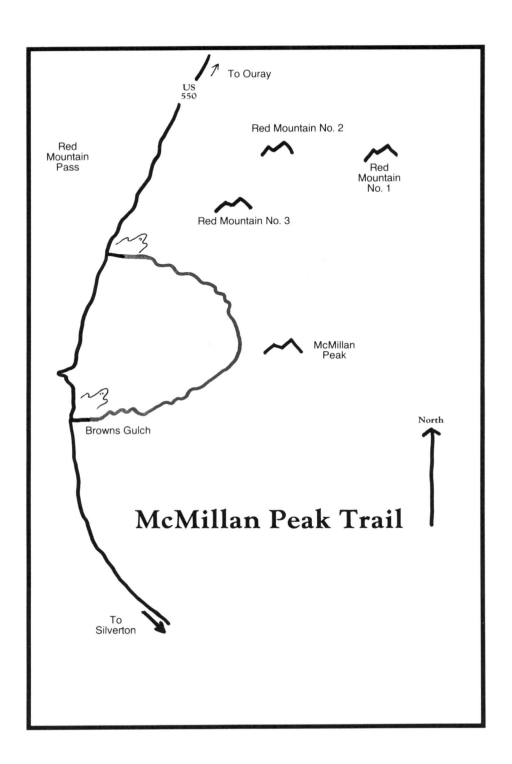

To Ouray

US
550

Red Mountain No. 2

Red
Mountain
No. 1

Red
Mountain
Pass

Red Mountain No. 3

McMillan
Peak

Browns Gulch

North

McMillan Peak Trail

To
Silverton

282

McMILLAN PEAK

McMillan Peak is an attractive but not spectacular 12,800-foot mountain in the San Juan range that offers a particularly fine panoramic view from its broad summit. The mountain lies north of Silverton but south of Red Mountain Pass and east of US 550. It is shown on both the Silverton and Ironton quadrangle maps published by the U.S. Geological Survey. The trail, however, is not shown on either of these fine maps.

If you approach this area from the north you should cross Red Mountain Pass, continuing south past the site of the ghost town of Chattanooga below the curve, then continuing for an additional mile and a half. Here you will find the beginning of a four-wheel-drive road that runs east or left up Browns Gulch. Since this is not one of the popular Jeep roads, our experience has been that traffic of that type is rare on this trail, but it is always a possibility.

Beginning at an elevation of approximately 10,000 feet, the trail executes a series of climbing switchbacks up through a dense growth of evergreen and deciduous trees. At approximately 11,700 feet the trail swings gradually around to the north. It emerges above the forest at roughly 11,800 feet, following a grassy but treeless ridge to McMillan Peak and its grand view. From nearly any angle or direction, the scenery is outstanding, particularly to the west and northwest.

If you can arrange with a patient friend to pick you up, the trail does go on to the north from the summit. It emerges through the old and little known ghost town of Summit onto Red Mountain Pass just south of its top. Barring such transportation arrangements you should return either by the trail on which you came up, or by walking down US 550 past the foot of the pass to your car.

San Juan
AREA

From the top of McMillan Peak we look toward a section of the
magnificent San Juan Range.

Bear Mountain is the pointed peak at the center of this panorama
from McMillan Peak.

For this hike, mid-July through September would be the preferred times. Although we have never tried it, we suspect that this area would be very pretty when the aspens change color.

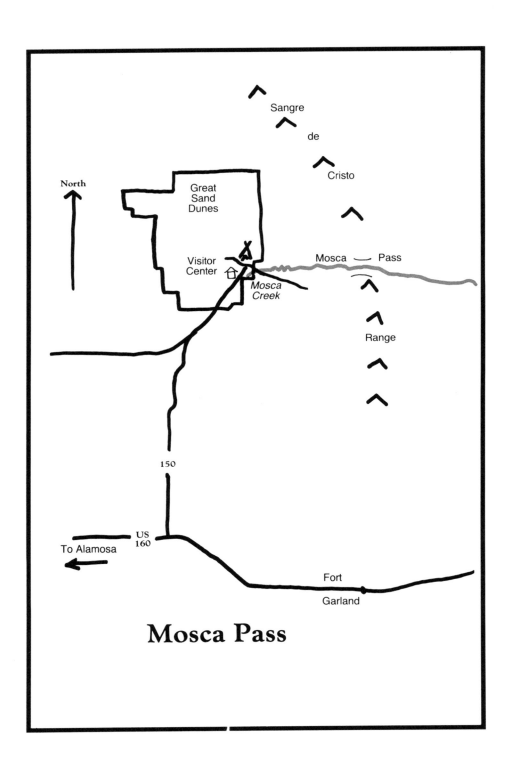

North

Sangre
de
Cristo

Great
Sand
Dunes

Visitor
Center

*Mosca
Creek*

Mosca — Pass

Range

150

US
160

To Alamosa

Fort
Garland

Mosca Pass

286

MOSCA PASS

As early as the eighteenth century, 9,713 foot high Mosca Pass was used by people for crossing the Sangre de Cristo mountains. It is a fascinating place for the hiker and for the student of history. In the beginning, this crossing was used as an Indian trail. Later it was taken over by the Spanish who improved it. It was already a well-established route when the Zebulon M. Pike expedition explored its west side after they supposedly had crossed nearby Medano Pass during the winter of 1806–07. More recent research suggests that the Pike party actually crossed Mosca rather than Medano Pass. Those landmarks described in Pike's journal are not visible from any of the viewpoints on Medano Pass, but they are readily seen from Mosca's west side.

Next to come was the French trader Antoine Robideau (Robidoux) who took wagons across the trail as early as 1825. Robideau carried on a brisk trade in furs and supplies between his Santa Fe–Taos base and the Utah territory. Inevitably, his trail became known as Robideau's Pass. He continued to use it through the 1830s to reach his Fort Uncompahgre on the Gunnison River near present Delta. Supposedly he transported his goods in two wheeled carts. Incidentally, Antoine spelled his name Robidoux when he scratched it on a rock in eastern Utah in 1837 (see accompanying photograph).

In 1848 John C. Fremont, the famed "Pathfinder," used Robideau's crossing in his ill-fated winter search for a transcontinental railroad route. If usable snow-free valleys could be found, he reasoned, summer railroading would be easy. By 1853 we were still looking since Congress had appropriated $150,000 to finance four more surveys to locate a feasible cross country route.

San Juan
AREA

John W. Gunnison led the first try. He examined and rejected Robideau's Pass as being too steep before he and seven of his men were massacred, possibly by Paiute Indians, in Utah. Some months after Gunnison's death, Fremont retraced most of Gunnison's route, including this pass, to complete the survey.

Later in the century a town called Montville grew up at the western foot of the pass. Its general store and the post office were still there as late as 1898. By this time, the name of the pass had been changed to Mosca, a Spanish word for "fly." Briefly, the name was anglicized as Fly Pass. The name was an appropriate one. We once tried this hike in June and were so inundated by insects that we turned back. Mosca Pass was a toll road from 1871 until its charter was purchased by the state. One of the original toll gate posts is still visible at the Montville site.

When the aspens and cottonwoods turn to gold in late autumn, this becomes one of the most colorful hikes in all of Colorado. In fact, we rate it as our number one choice. To enjoy this lovely walk, drive north from Alamosa or south from Poncha Pass to Great Sand Dunes National Monument. Plan on a chilly night in the campground and prepare accordingly.

The Montville Nature Trail starts at a northeast point across the road from the Visitor's Center. Park here and begin walking east on the so-called Montville Trail. Where it curves around to the northwest, take the right fork. Cross Mosca Creek on the bridge and begin the three and a half mile climb to the top. The steepest part of the grade occurs in the first mile and a half. Here too the trail is somewhat open as you make your way east up the canyon wall. When you have gained some elevation, pause to look back at the sand dunes.

Rather quickly you will enter an area of dense vegetation where yellow aspens and cottonwoods stand out against the darker evergreens. Red scrub oak is abundant here too. Although autumn colors vary in Colorado from year to year, we have found the most brilliant hues here during the first weekend in October. Looking at this

At one time, the historic Mosca Pass Trail was an important wagon road over the Sangre de Cristo Mountains.

One view of the Mosca Pass Trail looks back toward Great Sand Dunes and the San Luis Valley.

In 1837 Antoine Robidoux announced his intent to establish a trading post on the Winte (Uinta) River. Robidoux's Rock still exists but is difficult to find.

hiking path today, it is difficult to imagine a wagon road traversing Mosca Canyon.

Now the grades become more gentle and a lovely meadow opens up just ahead. Painted marker posts have been placed along the trail at half mile intervals. Just before you reach the three mile post, a second trail comes in from the right. Avoid this and continue walking straight ahead. Soon you will enter a second meadow and the end of the trail is at the top of the next ridge.

The sturdy fence ahead of you has been erected to keep motorized traffic off the hiking path. At the top of the pass, a graded road comes up from Gardner in the Wet Mountain Valley. We usually backtrack here and have lunch among the trees before returning to the Sand Dunes by the same route.

Although summer hikes are popular on Mosca Pass, obviously we prefer the autumn season when the temperatures are brisk and the leaves have attained their fullest color saturation. As described here the total walking distance, round trip, is just under eight miles with approximately 2,200 feet of elevation gain. Again, be sure to carry a camera.

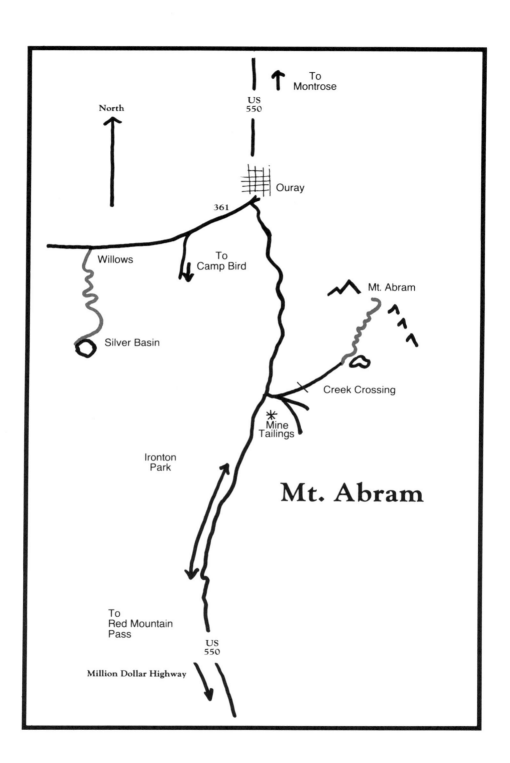

North

To
Montrose

US
550

Ouray

361

Willows

To
Camp Bird

Mt. Abram

Silver Basin

Creek Crossing

Mine
Tailings

Ironton
Park

Mt. Abram

To
Red Mountain
Pass

US
550

Million Dollar Highway

MOUNT ABRAM

Although some people persist in calling this peak both Mount Abrams and "Father Abraham," its correct name is Mount Abram. It was named for Abram Cutler, the notary public who administered the oath to Ouray's first town board. Cutler Creek, north of Ouray, also bears his name. Mr. Cutler built a road known as the Cutler Cutoff that connected the towns of Cimarron and Colona. Because he assisted Ferdinand Vandiveer Hayden with his notable survey of 1874, it has been said that Hayden named the peak in his honor. Curiously, the name does not appear on Hayden's map. So we do not know who named this handsome 12,801 foot high prominence for Abram Cutler.

Mount Abram dominates the skyline south of Ouray. Viewed from the north, it becomes the central point for one of the most photographed vistas in Colorado. Its steep slopes have led climbers to conclude that "there is no easy way up Abram." In his fine book, *Guide to the Colorado Mountains*, my friend Robert M. Ormes describes the steep approach up the west slope from a point in the north end of Ironton Park. It is a challenging climb.

The route described here was shown to us by Earl and Barbara Boland of Ouray and Golden. It too begins in Ironton Park, but if you have access to a 4-wheel drive vehicle, several hundred feet of elevation gain can be eliminated. Even as a pedestrian venture, this climb involves a greater distance than the Ormes route, but the grades are more gradual.

As you enter Ironton Park from the north, drive to the huge tailings dump on the east side of the road and turn left or east on the dirt road that skirts the north extremity of the dump. Almost at once the road forks in

The dim trail to Mt. Abrams can be seen from a point near the timberline. The peak itself shows on the center horizon.

This view looks north from the summit of Mt. Abrams. The white line that wanders toward the top of the picture is US Highway 550.

three directions. Keep to the left here, cross the creek and continue up the trail. You are now on Brown Mountain. Several switchbacks will take you up through a heavily wooded hillside to a point near timberline. Now the road forks at a tiny lake. Here you should keep to the left. Where the trail ends, look straight ahead of you to the north. The zig-zag switchbacks on the shoulder of the mountain are the start of this trail. At this point the elevation is about 11,600 feet.

Be especially watchful as you start up this trail. It is very narrow and indistinct. It slopes off in the wrong direction and the drop-off below you is impressive. This condition persists for about three-quarters of a mile, then it levels out a bit as the path traverses an above timberline meadow. Mount Abram is the most northerly prominence of the ridge that rises on your right as you continue uphill.

Now you must leave the narrow path and begin climbing upward along the steep eastern ridge. Avoid the patches of scree rock; they are dangerous on a hillside as steeply angled as this one. No trail exists on this grade, but it is easy to see where you must go. When you reach the ridge there is a dim path that follows the contour all the way north to the summit of Mount Abram.

From the top the vista is superb. Ouray can be seen to the north while Poughkeepsie Gulch is off to the east. Many spectacular peaks surround you on the horizon. The return is by the same route. Watch your landmarks carefully as you descend. The preferred season for this climb would be from late July through autumn. Avoid this trek at all costs in bad weather. The walking distance will be just over five miles. Truly, there is no easy way up Mount Abram.

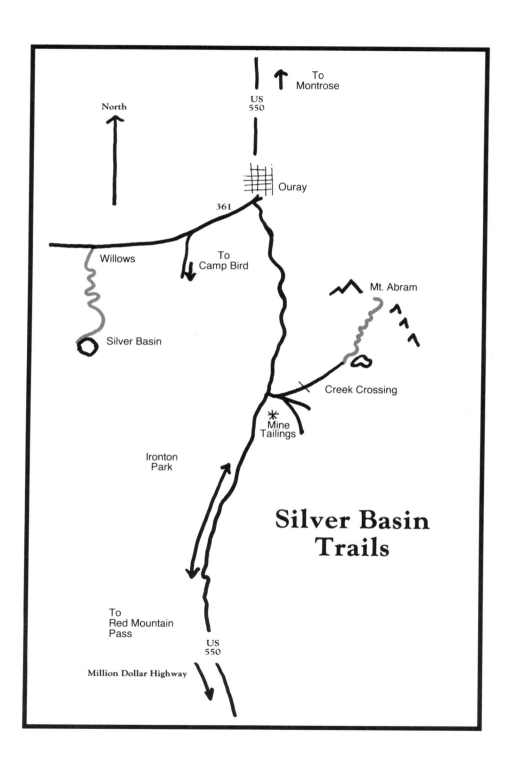

To
Montrose

US
550

North

Ouray

361

Willows

To
Camp Bird

Mt. Abram

Silver Basin

Creek Crossing

Mine
Tailings

Ironton
Park

Silver Basin
Trails

To
Red Mountain
Pass

US
550

Million Dollar Highway

SILVER BASIN

Silver Basin is a delightful little gem of a place that lies deep in the San Juan mountains. It is both a remote and a ruggedly beautiful setting with a tiny turquoise blue lake. The lake is nestled in a sylvan glade beneath jagged, snaggle-topped peaks. The walking distance from the road is not great but the trail is steep, ascending from an elevation of about 10,400 feet to 11,700 in less than two miles.

Begin the trek at the south edge of the picturesque little city of Ouray on US 550. Take the unpaved County Road 361 southwest for five steep miles up to the Camp Bird Mine. At the junction the left fork goes into Camp Bird, but the right fork is the one you want. It continues climbing upward to the west, skirts under hanging rock and becomes a bumpy ledge road nearly to the ghost town of Sneffels, but you will not go all the way. Instead, watch for a dim, barely visible trail that leaves the road to the left and cuts through a bank of willows. Unless changed by the Uncompahgre National Forest, this is the only left turn between Camp Bird and Sneffels. Park here and begin walking.

Just below the road is Canyon Creek, and you will need to cross it. Canyon Creek is both cold and swift but is not particularly deep. Originally this trail was blazed to facilitate transportation to and from a now abandoned silver mine. The path is double rutted, often muddy and steep. It negotiates a series of switchbacks up through groves of massive evergreen trees. The U.S. Geological Survey Ironton quadrangle map shows this as a pack trail.

When you reach the vividly tinted lake, stop and use your camera. Although the lake has no official name, some Ouray people refer to it as Lake Barbara. The

This is the somewhat remote location known as Silver Basin.

Silver Basin is surrounded by jagged ridges.

abandoned mine is not visible from the lake. To see it, continue up the trail for another quarter of a mile. A single building with what appears to have been a wooden sheathed chimney sits atop a medium-sized ore dump.

Your return is by the same route. By the time you reach your car, you will have walked between three and four miles. Try the Silver Basin hike only in late summer or early autumn, before the first snows fall. As a snowshoe trail, forget it. In winter the Canyon Creek road is one of the most treacherous snowslide areas in North America.

Silver Lake Trail

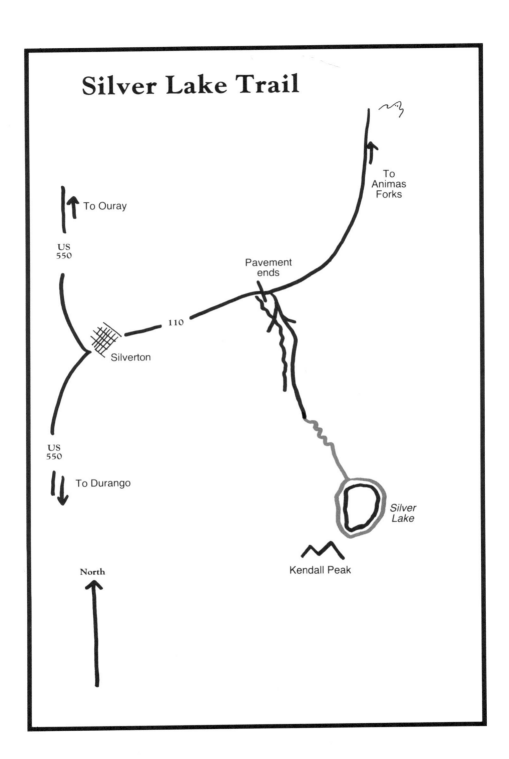

To Ouray

US
550

Pavement
ends

To
Animas
Forks

110

Silverton

US
550

To Durango

Silver
Lake

Kendall Peak

North

SILVER LAKE

Although Silver Lake is a rare gem of alpine beauty, we do not recommend this trail to the novice. Our hope is that you will read about it and then forget it. Access is difficult, there is danger from rock slides, the trail itself is steep, rocky and narrow. In short it was never used as anything except a pack trail. It is shown on the U.S. Geological Survey quadrangle map for Howardsville. If you are at all apprehensive about heights when there's little to stand on, avoid this trail.

If you are still determined to visit Silver Lake here are the directions. Drive north east from Silverton on County Road 110 for 2.4 miles. At this writing the pavement ends here. Now turn right and drive south east up Arastra Gulch. Go left at the only junction. The season, the weather, and what you are driving will determine the point at which you begin walking. With a 4-wheel drive it is possible to agonize all the way up the steep, rocky ledge to the burned out remains of the Mayflower Mine. At timberline, as you approach the head of the gulch, look sharply up to your left. The large structures clinging to the sheer rock wall are what remain of the Mayflower.

The distance from County Road 110 to the mine is approximately three miles. Where the road ends, above the surviving buildings, there is a cramped parking area for about four vehicles. The hiking trail to Silver Lake starts behind the charred timbers, between them and the sheer rock wall. Try to arrange for an early start as the trail remains in shade until late in the forenoon, and the coolness helps.

The "V" shaped, rock-filled structures beside the trail were used to break up rock avalanches and snowslides that would otherwise have destroyed the aerial tram towers. We have seen one rockslide on this trail, so be cautious. From the slide breakers to the town and lake is about two more miles. The path emerges onto a high meadow through a low place in the lip of the wall. Having reached this point the worst is over. Now follow the dim path that wanders across a succession of rolling, treeless hillocks. This is an easy path to lose, so head generally uphill into the basin.

Silver Lake lies at an elevation of 12,200 feet. Geologically, it is a natural glacial tarn. Curiously, since the basin was found to have been heavily mineralized, there were three large mines and two smaller ones along the lake's shoreline. Parts of three big mills still stand. The largest of these was the Silver Lake. Beyond it, on the west side, stood the Iowa. The Royal Tiger was across the lake from the Iowa. A dim but quite pleasant foot path circles the entire lake. In July the wild flowers are a blanket of bright colors. At the far end of the lake the most prominent mountain is 13,451 Kendall Peak, not to be confused with nearby Kendall Mountain.

Silver Lake was discovered and developed by the Stoiber Interests in the early 1880s. In 1903 it was sold to the Guggenheims. An aerial tramway transported the raw ore down in buckets to the great Silver Lake mill, a huge gravity feed structure that stood beside the Animas River near the mouth of Arastra Gulch.

Since rain dislodges boulders, do not attempt to hike to Silver Lake when the weather appears threatening. If there is a "better" season for this trail it would be late summer through early autumn. Incidentally, Silver Lake claimed the record for the greatest twenty-four hour snowfall. On April 14, 1920, seventy-six inches of snow fell in a single day. The storm continued into the following day. By the time seventy-two hours had elapsed, a total of ninety-eight inches had fallen. In all, the storm lasted for eighty-five hours. When it ended, one hundred inches was the measured depth. So watch the weather carefully before you start up the trail to picturesque Silver Lake.

The narrow, rocky pack trail to Silver Lake has changed but little.

Kendall Peak appears beyond Silver Lake.

Elk are common in Colorado's high mountains in summer. When
winter arrives, they migrate down to warmer valleys.

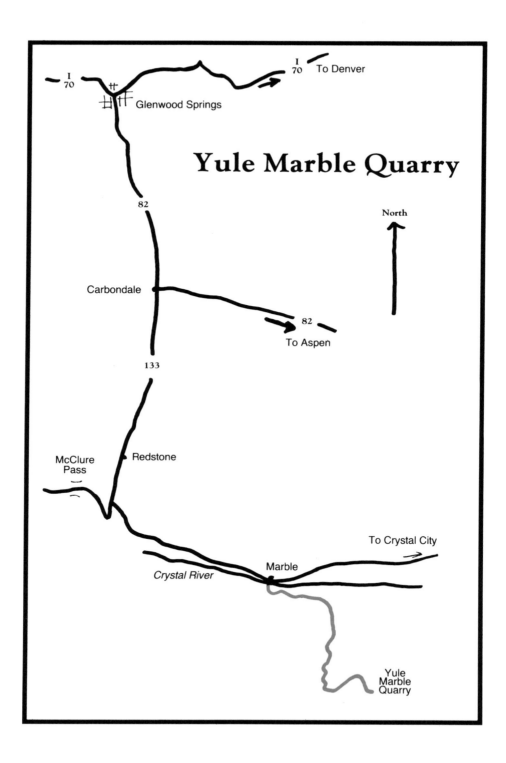

Yule Marble Quarry

North

I 70 — To Denver

I 70

Glenwood Springs

82

Carbondale

82 — To Aspen

133

McClure Pass

Redstone

To Crystal City

Marble

Crystal River

Yule Marble Quarry

The YULE MARBLE
QUARRY TRAIL

In common with so many of the walks described within these pages, this is another one with a rich history. Prospectors found gold in the Crystal Valley in the 1870s and small mining settlements grew up at Scofield, Crystal City, and at Clarence, near Marble. Then it was found that nearby Treasure Mountain was virtually a solid mass of the finest grade of white quarrying marble. Its quality and texture rivaled the Vermont deposits. The rich find quickly altered the economic base and the identity of the little town of Clarence, which became Marble.

To follow the Quarry Trail, drive southeast from Glenwood Springs on State Highway 82 to Carbondale. Turn south on State Highway 133, following the Crystal River through Redstone. Go left at the next junction and on to Marble. As an alternative, from Aspen you can follow State Highway 82 northwest to Carbondale, then up the river as described.

Since Marble still enjoys a small summer population, anyone in town can direct you to the place where the Quarry trail begins. It is probably easier to ask at Dave Jones' store. The trail, a road at this point, crosses the Crystal River and starts uphill along a lateral grade to the south. Before the grade changes direction there are good views of the town and of the foundations of the Colorado Yule Marble Company's Finishing Plant that stood beside the river until well into the present century. Here the marble was planed and finished into columns, blocks, and other fanciful shapes.

For a long time this trail was extensively used by 4-wheel drive vehicles. In recent years it has been closed to all except foot and horse traffic. It is a generally easy

Looking back from the trail to the Yule Quarry, the town of Marble
can be seen in the valley below.

At the mouth of the quarry there are huge blocks of lovely white
marble, even today.

grade, narrow in places, wet and eroded here and there. It is not steep. To the quarry, the distance is about two miles. Although high transportation costs and the development of synthetics killed the marble business in Colorado, you will note upon reaching the quarry that there is no shortage of this fine material. Even now there are huge blocks with rusting metal cables still attached, waiting for the transportation that will never come again.

In addition to the Washington Monument, a generous number of civic buildings came from the Yule Quarry. The world's largest block of marble ever taken from the ground in one piece came up from this enormous cavity. After cutting and polishing, it now stands in Arlington National Cemetery as the Tomb of the Unknown Soldier. We have been told that a second block of identical size was cut as a spare, in case the first one broke. According to our source it still lies deep in the quarry, accessible by a dark and very wet tunnel that goes in from the river, but we have never seen it. Above the quarry, a short walk will take you up to a group of precariously located frame buildings. This was Quarrytown, where the predominantly Italian laborers lived in order to be close to their work.

Rock slides and snow avalanches are not unknown here, and the frequency of mud slides has been all too common. In 1941 a massive wall of mud buried a substantial part of Marble. Our recommendation for this scenic four mile round trip walk is summer or autumn. In late September the aspen trees turn to gold up here. Few Colorado locations can surpass the Crystal Valley for autumn colors. Take a camera, a wide angle lens, and plenty of film.